NEIGHBORHOOD POWER

Oct. 10 Fri. morning
5:00 am

1-82

John

P.O. 6682
River Stat.
Rochester, NY
    19627

Neighborhood Power
The New Localism

David Morris and Karl Hess

Beacon Press  *Boston*

Library of Congress Cataloging in Publication Data

Morris, David J
  Neighborhood power.
    Bibliography: pp. 173–177
    1. Cities and towns—Planning—United States.
  2. Neighborhood.   I. Hess, Karl, 1923–   joint
author.   II. Title.
HT167.M67   309.2'62'0973   74–16663
ISBN 0–8070–0874–5
ISBN 0–8070–0875–3 (pbk.)

For our neighbors

Acknowledgments

We would like to thank, above all, our co-workers and neighbors at Community Technology and the Institute for Local Self-Reliance for generating many of the ideas, and not a little of the data, that have gone into this book. If it weren't for the residents of the Adams Morgan community growing vegetables on their roofs, mapping out the neighborhood for urban food production, setting up cooperative businesses, talking about small-scale technology, building solar cookers, starting neighborhood assemblies, hosting block parties, having fun, we might never have believed in the practicability of neighborhood power.

Thanks to Therese Hess for doing a superb job of editing a messy manuscript, and to Mary Jo Sutherland, for doing an equally superb job of urging it on to completion as the beautiful summer months beckoned.

A special thanks to Gil Friend and Neil Seldman. Many long hours of dialogue with them helped to refine vague and crude ideas.

Needless to say, the authors alone are responsible for the statements in this book. It's up to other neighborhoods and small cities around the country to add their own chapters to the growing literature of local efforts at self-reliance and independence.

Contents

NEIGHBORHOOD POWER

ONE

Neighborhoods: The Space to Be

A sense of neighborhood haunts our history and our fondest memories.

The neighborhood of childhood, whether a place to flee in rage or a place to remember in mellowness, is the location of heroic deeds, of epic villains, of home. When people say "where I grew up," they usually mean that early neighborhood where children at play took the first steps toward being grown-ups at work.

Later, of course, the sense of neighborhood is put to more severe testing. When people then say "my neighborhood," it usually means they have found a place to live where they feel some human sense of belonging, some human sense of being *part of a society,* no matter how small, rather than just be___ *in* a society, no matter how large. But, then, people can just as easily say simply "where I live," as though it is merely a rest stop on a road full of such stops, with each one merging into the next so hazily that it takes handfuls of old bills to even remember where you've been. Neighborhoods are memorable. A jumble of "places" where you've lived is not.

Those neighborhoods can be seen as simply neighborhoods of sentiment. They are the neighborhoods people talk about. Cynics say they are never neighborhoods in which people actually live. They are memories; and that's all.

But behind the memories there must be *some* reality. And, of course, there is. Most Americans live in neighborhoods. In small towns, the neighborhoods may be as simple as "over town" or "south" or "across the tracks," or any other of the thousand and one ways in which even the smallest of towns divide their clumps of people and housing, sometimes even businesses, into areas which have some distinct things in common — topography, ethnicity, class, or longevity (the old part of town as distinct from the new). In slightly larger towns the neighborhoods may themselves be conglomerates of types of people, classes, and races, but held together or made distinct by sheer geography or some division that separates the town or city — a highway, a river, or what have you.

By the time we get to cities, the neighborhoods may exhibit every one of those distinguishing marks — an ethnic neighborhood here, an income-level neighborhood there, an historic neighborhood there, a housing development that has been around long enough to *seem* like a neighborhood, or a cultural neighborhood (the arty place, the hippy place, the skid row).

In the cities, also, there is another very widespread characteristic of neighborhoods: many of them existed previously as independent municipalities. (Brooklyn was a major American city once, not just a part of New York City; Georgetown was a thriving river port and city, not just a part of Washington, D.C.; Roxbury was a city, not just a district of Boston.) Annexation, characteristically, ended the separate municipal status of these places, merging them into the city. Few if any went willingly. The most familiar pattern of annexation is that the citizens of the independent municipality resist year after year. But eventually the effort becomes wearisome. The votes get closer. Finally, as though in sheer exhaustion, the independent municipality gives up and becomes just another part of the big city. What was once a small town now becomes a big-city neighborhood.

Neighborhoods, therefore, have history. Do they have anything else? Do they have any practical meaning in what is called an age of complexity and an age that demands such vastness of social scale as to make mere neighborhoods seem like fossil relics of some societal Stone Age?

Major social critics and social planners say that the neighborhoods are just that, fossil relics. They say that neighborhoods are outdated. In the jet age we can settle for nothing less than global concepts (global villages, for instance) with no room left for merely human-sized communities.

Throughout the twentieth century the scale of social organization has been moving away from and not toward the scale of neighborhoods. Not even nation-states are big enough any more. International business combines arise to crisscross borders. International pacts join nations for this or that purpose. Even trade unions grasp at the vision, calling themselves "internationals" when given the least excuse — having members in Canada as well as the United States.

The neighborhood, if not simply scoffed at in this new globalism, is actually reviled and rejected. Neighborhood customs are somehow inevitably petty and even vicious, the critics say. Their alternative, of course, is the customs of great states, mighty nations, and efficient central governments. Yet, these same institutions wage devastating wars, are everywhere at odds with their own citizenry, torn by internal stresses, and increasingly viewed as absolutely incapable of decently regulating the lives of the millions over whom they claim sovereignty. It is true enough, of course, that neighborhood customs can be petty, vicious, cruel, even barbarous. But it is not true — as it is so obviously true with all larger institutions — that the meanness or violence can spread as efficiently as from a larger, more powerful source. A neighborhood of violence is still a neighborhood. A nation, suddenly embarked upon violence, is potentially a world calamity, a conflagration.

Still the critics persist. If neighborhoods had any sort of independence, might they not defy the worthy goals of the greater political leaders, the national leaders? Of course they might. But how better judge the wisdom of a larger political goal than by whether or not the people involved will actually support it? Isn't democracy, as a matter of fact, founded upon that sort of test? And where might people better discuss and decide their support of and role in larger political actions than in the one place where they can debate among themselves, as citizens — in their own neighborhoods?

But yet, the neighborhood may simply be an impractical

size of territory for the provision of those services which are deemed the heart of city life: trash collection, police protection, and fire protection. The critics of small-scale social organization all say that is the case. They claim that there are vast economies of scale to be gained by having single departments, covering great areas, to do essential work.

Today, the boasted economies of scale in our large cities are hardly even to be taken seriously after a common-sense look around us. Police departments, huge and depersonalized, are far removed from the days of the policeman who was our protector, friend, and neighbor. One result has been a wave of scandals which continues to rock major cities. The other is the growing sense that big-city police forces are simply incapable of dealing with ordinary street crime — that only action at the neighborhood level can do the job.

Trash collection has been turned over to technocrats who imagine that everything can be solved by just buying a larger piece of machinery. The result is great dinosaur-like vehicles which roam the streets, apparently eager to devour every bit of trash in sight and yet, because of their size, almost unable to move on smaller streets, virtually excluded from alleys, and so hard to start, stop, and even to feed with trash that they leave behind them a familiar wake of scattered waste, too small for such grand machinery to bother with, but day by day an accumulating nuisance. Are streets cleaner now that the machines are bigger and the bureaucracies controlling them bigger? The answer is obvious. No.

Fire departments are among the most vital local services and, of all services, have remained closest to neighborhood size in scale of operations, in scale of machinery (this machinery *must* be maneuverable), and in scale of unit organization. A firehouse is itself a small neighborhood of cooperative people.

Now, however, critics of neighborhood independence, particularly of the independence of neighborhoods in big cities, say that a neighborhood couldn't support a fire department! Yet most "neighborhoods" with fire departments out and around the countryside are in fact smaller places than most big-city neighborhoods. Big-city neighborhoods are populated densely, with ten to thirty thousand people not being uncommon. Those are, in fact, the sizes of small towns, actually of what many might call medium-sized towns. And those towns all have fire departments. The smaller ones, to be sure, rely on some volunteers as well as on professionals. Big-town fires are more demanding, but the fact remains that even in big towns, the application of so-called economies of scale does not seem actually productive of better services in essential areas.

Final proof of the failure of the so-called economies of scale lies in the simple fact that the rise of great city problems and the rise of great city political power have proceeded side by side. The larger the power and scope of city administrations, the larger the problems. This is not to say that the large size of the city administrations caused the problems. It is to say that the increase in the scale of city administration has not solved those problems. It also is to say that the increase in the scale of city administration has not ushered in an era of smaller budgets. Quite the contrary. The economy of scale does not produce an economy-sized budget after all. But when all is said and done, isn't everything just caused by the fact that cities are getting bigger and bigger? Hardly. Some are losing population. The scale of city administrations, by any measure, has outpaced the increase in scale of population.

Yet the neighborhoods, many of them, persist. It is the contention of this book, throughout, that they do not persist merely as fossils, as sentimental areas, or as fortresses of special interest or prejudice. Most persist, and all could be revived, for the simply practical reasons of making life livable and resolving problems which have remained untouched by the movement toward huge, dehumanized scale in social organization, economic organization, and in the organization of resources and technology.

Neighborhoods deserve and are getting new attention for supremely important reasons — not simply because neighborhoods may be practical but because they may be necessary. It may be necessary to revive and live in neighborhoods or face the possibility of simply having no place else to go.

In big cities, the institutions of larger scale which have

marked city growth are clearly falling apart. The quality of life in every big city of America — and perhaps of the entire world — is being seriously questioned and being seriously described as deteriorating. At the same time the relationship of working people to the work they do is also falling apart, leaving more frustrations, less sense of accomplishment and meaning, more trash and less craft, more quantity and less quality. And around it all, the sense of citizenship is falling into a cynical decline. Politicians are expected to be corrupt and people generally expect that there is nothing to be done about it. A civic weariness has set in. There seems no real use to voting. The rascals all turn out the same. There seems little use to fighting city hall. The occupants all turn out to be the same. And so, people's heads turn toward—— what? Toward home. Toward where they live. How they live. Going home, in this sense, means rediscovering the neighborhood.

What is the neighborhood? It is place and it is people. It has no defined size or even scale, although common-sense limits do appear throughout history. The homeliest tests for neighborhood would include the fact that a person can easily walk its boundaries. It is not so large that going from one side to another requires special effort. Its physical size means that it is or can be familiar turf for everyone in it. Its boundaries arise often out of history. Some original purpose of settlement brought people to this particular spot which may have been then a particular spot in an area already being settled. It might have been chosen for no more complicated reason than that it was an available and unoccupied piece of land. It might have been chosen because it resembled some other familiar place. It might have been chosen so that newcomers could be close to older residents they respected, knew, or simply didn't fear. There might be a class base. Artisans might have gathered in one particular part of a growing town area. Laborers in another. Clerks in another. Students, of course, might create a neighborhood around a school. Ethnic groups might choose to live together. Religious groups might do the same.

Neighborhoods continue to spring up, whether in small towns or in urban centers. People know the extent of the neighborhood. In a way it could be said that neighborhoods are self-defining. They are defined by the people who live in them. People know when they are in their neighborhood and they know when they are out of it. You or we probably would be hard pressed to define technically any neighborhood. Yet, once in one, we would know it. People might tell us. We might sense it from the style of life or houses, or streets — or from any of many other external signs.

The importance of the neighborhood begins with the importance of citizenship. To be a citizen is to participate in civic affairs. "Participate" is the key concept. To simply live in a place, and not participate in its civil affairs, is to be merely a resident, not a citizen. It is pointed out incessantly in political-science discourses that not everybody wants to be a citizen. The chore of participation is said to be beyond the energy or the skill of most people.

To the modern liberal disposition this means that central planning, powerful executive-type government, and technocratic elites are justified and, indeed, necessary in running a society "efficiently."

To the modern conservative disposition this means a justification of hard class lines in society (the poor will always be with us, the rich will rise to the top naturally) and also justifies a corporate system which, by providing everything for people, makes it unnecessary for people to bother about anything but consuming — and showing up for work on time.

To both major political dispositions, the idea of citizenship as participation is unacceptable. The liberal wants citizenship to mean support of the government. The conservative wants citizenship to mean support of the corporations and as little government as possible — except for the government needed to support business!

For anyone who sees a different importance to citizenship or who feels that participation in political life is not only possible but desirable for all people, there is the immediate question of *where* the politics will be practiced. To ask just *how* is to open the door to the past and close it to the future. Past political emphasis always has been on "how" citizenship would be exercised. From that preoccupation has grown the entire system in which citizenship is exercised by representation. Citizens elect others to perform their civil or political chores. That is said to be efficient. It also is said to be a solution to how citizenship may be exercised by millions of people. It presupposes that it is necessary for them to exercise that citizenship all together, toward united goals. It is the prime requisite of the big nation-state and, in fact, it requires that people be more like residents in the nation-state than actual citizens. The citizens do not debate and propose, they simply ratify or reject. And, no matter how lustily the rhetoric of any such nation-state may proclaim the equality of all citizens, it is obvious to anyone's common-sense observation that some citizens are far more equal than others. The class of citizens whose work is politics exercise citizenship on behalf of all the rest. They *are* political citizens. The others in the society are simply political constituents.

It is impossible to say that such a system does not work. Of course it works. It works to support a very particular structure of politics, one with national goals and with national power. All other levels of interest are subordinate to those goals and power and, once again, the preoccupation of politics is with how to mesh the citizens into the structure.

For the foreseeable future, of course, the national nature of politics will continue to dominate all other politics. Citizenship will be, by and large, viewed as a means to choose among programs advanced by leaders. The best of politics will afford a chance to select the leaders (but, again, to make the selection from lists prepared — by leaders!). The worst will autocratically declare programs and then measure citizenship by how eagerly people turn out to work without having to be whipped or threatened.

Even so, while the familiar definitions of politics and citizenship persist, there are clear signs that interests in other definitions will grow. The collapse of so many functioning units of big government, even while government power grows to new scale, will, as mentioned earlier, be a major occasion for this interest. To survive the collapse of familiar institutions or even their slow decay, people will organize some affairs differently.

And the ones most likely to be organized differently will be the ones that *can* be organized differently. Those affairs, we contend, are the most local. They are the things that happen where people live. They are the things which bring us to a consideration of politics as not so much a question of "how" as a question of "where."

If the inclination is to give politics first a location rather than simply an abstract structure, entirely new political dynamics are begun.

The purpose of politics becomes more focused. The purpose is to make possible the peaceful living together of people who may be very temperamentally and culturally different, but who share a space. In this case the sharing of space is very specific. It does not mean the sharing of the planet which, of course, we all do but in such a different way than the way in which we share a neighborhood. It is possible to share the planet without ever seeing or even being aware of the existence of most other people on it. It is possible to share the planet, also, while being aware of everybody on it but, admittedly, that awareness is always a sort of abstraction since we never *know* all of the other people and, in fact, only in the most broad ecological sense do our lives ever really become intertwined. After saying, quite properly, that we are all human and share that humanness, and also share or should share a reverence for life, common sense would be hard pressed to say what concrete activity we all must share, all at once, all in the same way. The practical fact of the matter is that after our common humanity, we are a dazzlingly diverse bunch, with myriad interests and capabilities and cultures and styles and passions. A peaceful world might well be one simply in which all those differences are given space to be, without being allowed the power to force themselves on anyone else.

There is a special virtue of politics based on a small space, a space in which people can, by and large, know one another and share some sense of the place in which they live — and consequently share civic interests. The special virtue is that politics in a space of human scale — permitting face-to-face citizenship, so to speak — provides homes for diversity. A neighborhood can provide a home for people who are different from people in another neighborhood, in which case it would be seen as a homogenous neighborhood. There are many of them. Or it could provide a home for many different sorts of people all living together in one neighborhood, a heterogenous neighborhood. There are many of those, as well. The authors live in one like that and love it. Other people live in different sorts of neighborhoods, and many, presumably, love them just as well.

The emphasis is on the space itself and on establishing political activity within that space, rather than on abstract institutional politics in which sameness and uniformity become the goals of politics with diversity said to lie outside the political order and to be only cultural.

Yet the physical facts are overwhelming. People simply do not live in institutions or in areas of abstract political theory. The physical facts are that people live in particular places and work in particular places. People are not galactic atoms, floating in space. They walk on the earth. To try and locate politics in physical space is not some whim, it is a common-sense response to the physical facts of life. As an example: We all may be called Americans. We may, as things now stand, fully and enthusiastically share a sense of national purpose and national destiny and, when meeting foreigners particularly, we may emphatically say, "We are Americans." But the physical facts of our life are not so broad and abstract. We actually spend most of our time within the borders of that political subdivision called a state, one of the fifty. To people from other states we say, "I am a Virginian," or an Oregonian, or what have you. But the physical fact is even more exacting than that. We don't roam the state ceaselessly, living here and then living there. We live in a place. We say, finally, "I'm from Mineral Point" or "I'm from Johnstown" or "I'm from the Upper East Side." We actually know that even though we are Americans in abstract politics, we are people of a town or neighborhood. We live someplace.

The question is whether politics should also live there. Our point in this book is that yes, emphatically, politics should live there, where the people do. Our point is that it is practical for this to be, desirable for this to be, and that unless this is to be, there will not be a citizenship which also means the

freedom to participate. There will only and can only be citizen-
ships which mean at best the freedom at stated intervals to select
leaders.

It is our further contention that leaders are becoming
obsolete, that large-scale units of both the economy and politics
are actually social dinosaurs, lumbering toward a time when the
urgent demands of practical nature will make them extinct and
obsolete. Mineral resources will simply not support the waste and
concentrations of power which are the natural food of great
leadership. Rising aspirations of people generally to be more than
pawns in great power plans certainly challenge the ideas of great
and concentrated power. But, most of all, the simple and obvious
failures of great leaders and great powers to come to grips with
what really bothers people would seem to us to spell the slow
beginning of the long end of traditional, concentrated powers and
hierarchical leadership.

The source of the alternatives which could replace the old
orders of power, we feel, will be in the neighborhoods — not only
of this nation but of all nations — when people face real
necessities for alternative action and then see, in their neighborhoods, the space to take those actions.

Although this vision is turned squarely toward the future, it
is rooted very much in the past. The neighborhood is not some
panacea newly invented for a new crisis. The neighborhood *is* the
way people have lived historically throughout the world. The
neighborhoods have been the places, moreover, where people
have lived in relatively peaceful ways throughout history. It is not
from neighborhoods, either of artisans in cities or farmers in the
countryside, that wars and conflict emerge. The "neighborhood"
that engages in such enterprise is always the nation-state itself, or,
rather, the institutional seat of such a state — the palace, the
executive mansion, the whatever-you-call-it which claims the
broadest jurisdiction over a large territory and then maintains
armed power specifically to enforce that jurisdiction.

The neighborhood, at root, then, can be said to represent
the way people naturally live together. It does not represent a
political theory. It represents a human reality.

Beyond that, the neighborhood suggests a scale of living

together which enables people to represent their own interests, directly, face-to-face with all of the other people who may either share or be affronted by those interests. It is a political theory or, perhaps, presumption, to say that this is desirable. There is nothing absolutely natural about it, as there seems to be about the neighborhood itself. On the other hand, there is something sensible about it. Who else can best represent the interests of a person than that very person? Liberals say that smarter people can better represent everyone's interests. But that just means that the supposedly smarter people can *say* they better represent those interests. They certainly don't go out and interview everybody. They may assume that they don't have to do that because, after all, everyone is pretty much alike. But we know that is simply not true, from experience, and even the existence of the liberal, or elitist, position says clearly that they themselves don't believe we are all alike. They see themselves, at least, as different.

Conservatives seem to think that the more energetic and ambitious people can best represent all people, but conservatives have a special emphasis in which they suggest that the interests of people, after all, aren't so much political as they are simply acquisitive. People are said to be economic creatures interested only in creature comforts. Their interests, therefore, are best represented by the people who endlessly proliferate the soap flakes, cars, and candy which, the conservatives feel, are all that interest Americans anyway.

Our point is far different. Americans, like all people, are social. They enjoy living with, being with, working with, loving with, arguing with, and creating with and for other people. A few people, to be sure, just want to live off and alone. One of the problems today is that our entire society is structured as though everybody wants to live that way. Every part of the official structure, both corporate and political, encourages a concept of people as highly competitive, as wanting to be isolated, and as believing that their only hope for survival is to get what they can without reference to other people. Work roles are incredibly isolated and compartmentalized. The most profitable real-estate developments are those, like high-rise apartments, which crowd people together but in which there are no shared interests. Every part of life becomes separated by a maximum distance from every other part of life. Work here. Shop there. Vote here. Play someplace else. Have friends all over. Sleep there. Study here. And so forth.

Neighborhood life is the life that brings or tries to bring as much of human life together as possible. It is one special argument of this book, in fact, that in a new birth and building of neighborhood life, all human activity could be brought back together so that work, play, love, life, politics, science, and art could be a shared experience by people sharing a space, sharing agreements as to how to live together, and mutually aiding one another to enjoy the fullest, ripest existence as human beings in a humane setting.

The first steps toward that rebirth are being taken all across the country. There are literally thousands of examples — some are small and some substantial, some are clearly in a good direction while others might be argued about (but even disagreement can be viewed as a positive action in a stage of experimentation). This book is an attempt to pull together many of those widely varying experiences and synthesize them into some coherent form that will at least begin to show the who, what, why, when, where, and only then the how of the changes taking place. Of course, we have found it irresistible (as you should) occasionally to go beyond experience — to try to enlarge upon it, refine it, hybridize it — and make suggestions about things to be done which seem practical to us but which have not, to our knowledge, yet been tried. We think it is clear, throughout the following chapters, when we are talking about actual experiences and when we are speculating, *based on those experiences.*

We, the authors, have gained most of our personal experience where we live, in the Adams Morgan neighborhood in Washington, D.C. It is a neighborhood three-fourths of a mile square with a population of 30,000 people. It is mentioned often throughout the book, both because of our experiences here and because it is one of the more "developed" communities in the country in the sense that we discuss development in this book.

Although the book concentrates on big-city neighborhoods like ours, much of the experience we relate can be applied to smaller cities, suburban communities, and small towns. The face-to-face contact of big-city neighborhoods, plus the declining quality of services and increasing sense of frustration, seem to make these the first battlefields for local independence. But in some sense small towns and small cities, although not having the same intimacy as neighborhoods, have an added advantage because they possess juridical and economic power by being recognized subunits of states. This book is a call for a return to a human scale of organization, a return of power to the people affected by that power, and a return to a sense of community. The scale may well turn out to be much smaller than people have imagined. It seems to us not at all coincidental that ancient Greece and modern China have chosen as their basic political and economic units communities with populations no larger than many big-city neighborhoods. The argument that politics should be conducted on a local, face-to-face level is an old one, but new disciples of local control point out with increasing evidence that modern technology is itself decentralizing in its impact and that now, perhaps for the first time in history, we can begin to speak of efficient productive facilities as well on the local level.

This book describes a comprehensive process, always couched in localism, in the neighborhood. In succeeding chapters, we discuss ways to control local wealth, mechanisms for stabilizing land values, ways to establish community financial institutions, the potentials and limitations of neighborhood manufacturing. Throughout, we have tried to maintain the goal of local self-reliance and resident participation in decision-making.

A final caveat: this book is not an organizer's manual in the traditional sense. Most such manuals teach people what they can do to move against the centers of power and force them to change basic problems. We are interested, rather, in how we can positively re-create community within our neighborhoods. We treat neighborhoods, and the city, as underdeveloped nations. They now suffer from aspects of imperialism similar to those of the third-world countries: outside intervention in local affairs; absentee ownership; cultural dependency. While struggling to change these basic relationships, neighborhoods must also strive to develop, for themselves, new institutions, new relationships, new mechanisms for providing basic goods and services.

Since defense and reconstruction are part of the same process, we describe both. We emphasize, however, reconstruction: community housing rather than tenant unions; collectively owned food stores and neighborhood production facilities rather than consumer boycotts. Still, we are keenly aware that we cannot have a neighborhood at all if land developers use it as a way-station for downtown commuters or as the hub of a shopping-center district. We cannot compete effectively with Safeway or A&P on a neighborhood level. We cannot deal with the influence and power of multinational corporations by producing good merchandise in our small area. But we can learn together what life might be like if there were cooperation rather than competition. We can begin to gain a sense of self-confidence and self-reliance. And we can begin to plan and develop our communities, embracing the kind of diversity that is inherent in America's multi-ethnic and multi-racial population.

TWO

Developing Neighborhood Awareness: The First Institutions

Our neighborhoods are tiny, underdeveloped nations. They are owned, by and large, by outsiders who view them as profitable investments. Local money is put into financial institutions which invest it outside the local economy, often in competing industries. The communications networks are owned by multinational corporations, providing little news about domestic affairs and limiting the possibilities of internal communication or an exchange of information with like-minded "nations." Domestic news is secondary to international coverage; it is easier by far to know what is happening halfway around the world than in another part of our own neighborhood.

There is a parallel perversion of local customs and culture. Very little native art exists, primarily because it lacks access to conventional media channels. Those who own and operate the media do not understand native problems or culture. They are motivated by a desire for profits and the local economy is too small to provide a profitable market for their wares. Programming is geared to mass audiences and is slick, yet bland, and, above all, inoffensive, catering to the lowest common denominator.

The neighborhood, or little country if we follow that analogy, exports labor-intensive services and imports capital-intensive finished goods, paying out high prices for a technology generally unsuited to local conditions. There is little domestic industry and, where it does exist, it is supplied by foreign firms. The neighborhood is a net importer of goods and services, is always in debt, and, if it is a recognized political unit, keeps its head above water by taxing domestic businesses and residents' income, usually through regressive taxes, in order to maintain an inadequate welfare system.

Many neighborhoods are divided. Some people are rich and are allied with the foreign interests, often as minor partners. The middle class work as managers in the foreigners' firms, and try desperately to conform to the values of the upper class. The poor live on the edge of society, often surviving by entering into those sectors of the society declared illegitimate. Some neighborhoods seem to lack any common interest, merely share a common boundary. Although they all speak the same language, have similar customs, and are even physically familiar with one another, they do not view themselves as a community of interest.

The analogy could be pushed even further. Some neighborhood residents, seeing their colonial position today, can remember when the neighborhood was itself an independent city. Milton Kotler, in his classic book, *Neighborhood Government*, describes how city after city was subordinated to powerful downtown business interests during the last century, each giving up its power to enlarge a municipal area. Neighborhoods once had political power, but today have very little, and that only in those cities which are condemned for their machine politics and their ward bosses. In most cities even that semblance of identity has been eliminated with at-large elections of city officials.

Many, probably most, of the residents of big-city neighborhoods are not aware of their territorial history, or of their once independent status. Most do not yet accept that their growing impoverishment, both material and spiritual, comes from a lack of local control over affairs directly connected with local liberty and life. Yet, they know something is wrong. In various parts of the country neighborhoods are organizing, confronting municipal and national interests, defending their borders against land developers and highways, developing self-help institutions, demanding decentralized services, trying to control wealth created within the neighborhood and trying to produce more goods and services in the local area. And, as each step is taken, greater potentials are discovered. Where once people talked of little city halls, they are now talking about neighborhood manufacturing facilities. Where once people pushed for increased city services, they are now asking for taxes to be given directly back to the neighborhood for it to decide where they should be spent. Where once people asked banks not to declare their area off-limits for home mortgages, they are now exploring the possibilities of developing their own banking systems. Where once people were trying to stop utility-company rate increases, they are now demanding research into decentralized energy sources, so that neighborhoods can begin to break away from the large, isolated institutions.

Neighborhoods are a beehive of activity. Social matrices crisscross their territories. Corner grocery stores, local taverns and laundromats act as meeting places where neighborhood gossip and information is swapped. Civic associations are in evidence everywhere. Church groups and parent-teacher associations have regular meetings. Fraternal orders have their weekly bowling tournaments and not-so-secret meetings. And there are always local chapters of everything from the Democratic Party to the Cancer Association to the Boy Scouts.

No neighborhood is a blank slate. There are the remnants of old organizations, which have served their function and now serve a new one, that of a social vehicle for their elderly survivors. There are the more youthful and vibrant associations, flourishing under changing cultural conditions. And there are those established because of specific causes, such as the Vietnam War, or local food prices, or a national political campaign, which tend to fade rapidly after the issue leaves the front pages.

Most of these institutions serve as social vehicles, ways for people to come together, meet new friends, and share experiences. In some cases they make life more livable in the area. In rare instances they may be a part of the long network of the city, involved in local planning, writing up plans and programs for projects that may reach partial fulfillment a decade later, after they have wended their way through the city bureaucracy.

But rare are the institutions which are useful in creating an awareness of the possibilities and advantages of self-reliance. Rare are the organizations which attempt to go to the root of many of the neighborhood's problems — its dependency on outsiders who do not share its values and who have no sense of responsibility for the area. The development of awareness in a neighborhood is the creation of a consciousness both of the neighborhood's role in national life and of its ability to rely on its own resources to meet basic needs. As this attitude develops, previously untapped resources become highlighted. Vacant lots, side streets, libraries, schools, condemned buildings, all become potentially productive facilities for the area. A neighbor's skills are discovered and pooled with one's own to establish a primitive barter system for maintenance and construction within the perimeters of the neighborhood itself.

With this kind of change in attitude comes a subtle but significant change in one's relationship to the city itself. The struggle for neighborhood identity begins, and often follows this pattern: First, residents organize to maintain the integrity of their area against outside interests. Then, political mobilization of the neighborhood begins and there is an attempt to decentralize as much power as is possible from the city to the local unit. Finally, new institutions are established that will realize and reflect the kinds of economic, social, and personal relationships the neighborhood wants for itself. Each step produces its failures, its detours, its revisions. Yet with each step, the number of participants grows until finally the neighborhood reaches what the economists call the "take-off stage." In political and social terms this means the stage of development when there is a spontaneous and almost exponential growth in neighborhood organizations, pedestrian traffic within the area, and creativity in both stance and projects. The take-off stage is reached, for instance, when one can look back after a few years and say: "Wow, was this ever a dead neighborhood then. Now it seems like every week there is a new group planning something, starting a new store, opening a new service organization, petitioning the city about one thing or another, organizing another tenant union, creating a people's bank, publishing another community newsletter, putting on street theatre, designing street cutoffs, and on and on."

Yet in the beginning it seems difficult to imagine how the neighborhood will ever become so swollen with productive activity. In the beginning the major question is not how to *channel* this activity, but how to *initiate* it. And here we run up against the nature of neighborhoods, the nature of close and familiar living.

Neighborhoods are at one and the same time stabilizing and conservative. Their solid base of personal familiarity makes them the fundamental unit for democracy, yet that very familiarity and stability have given rise to a conservatism and caution which has produced the conventional wisdom that any democracy based on neighborhood power would be parochial, bigoted, and prejudiced. It is true that neighborhoods are often defensive and protective. It is a natural protectionism. With the world changing so rapidly, and the mass media illustrating how old value systems are crumbling, it is no wonder that neighbors try to build a wall around themselves. Residents try to protect their streets against the lawless, their schools against the truants, their kids against the drug pushers, their homes against the developers' bulldozers, their neighborhood theatres against the porno kings. Sometimes this protectionism runs rampant, becoming a defense against anything new. Anything that threatens the status quo — whether a shopping center or communal living arrangements, sex education in the schools or blacks moving into the area — is fought with equal zeal.

And, of course, over the long run a neighborhood cannot win defensive battles. A continuously defensive struggle is rarely victorious because it depends on the aggressor losing interest rather than on a shift in basic power relationships which would take away the aggressor's influence and authority. The neighborhood lacks political cohesion. It is not recognized as a unit of political power in most cities in the country. Decisions about local school curricula, zoning, subway stops, street designs, are all made by people mostly living outside the neighborhood. The vast majority of people who live in the neighborhood don't work there. The vast majority of those who own businesses in the neighborhood don't live there. In any planning decisions the neighborhood is more often viewed as a barrier to progress than as something to be preserved.

In terms of their relationship to their turf, there are three kinds of neighborhood residents: There are those, perhaps the majority, who have little connection either to the turf or to any vision of a reconstructed society. They do not work in the neighborhood, shop only rarely in its stores, and do not participate in neighborhood organizations. The next largest group are those who have deep roots in the neighborhood, who have participated in civic associations, who have lived there a long enough time to have a sense of historical continuity and a perspective on community changes. This group is usually older, although not always, and may have children and be property owners. Some of them have fought long and hard to make the neighborhood a viable place in which to live, and many may have retreated in frustration after having spent so much time and energy with so little result. Like the West Virginia small-town people, they might remember with some nostalgia great neighborhood struggles against the city or local developers. If the neighborhood is a working-class one, they can remember the violent struggles of the labor unions. If it is a black neighborhood, they might remember the struggles to integrate neighborhood facilities. That historical perspective and experience is quite important for the coming struggles and development.

Those with strong roots in the neighborhood often concern themselves with matters such as neighborhood beautification, trash removal, crime, barking dogs, and drug abuse. Many of their activities revolve around local church or educational or political organizations.

The third group is the "alternative community." Although they are usually young, their population is more accurately characterized by their ideological attitudes than their age. These are people who share a common value system but are not necessarily tied to the geographical neighborhood itself. Their sense of community flows from spiritual, social, racial, sexual, or ideological bonds.

Although "community" and "neighborhood" are used interchangeably for most of this book as words denoting the cluster of people who live in a specific geographic area, they are used differently here to explain two rather different strains of residents.

Here, neighborhood means a concrete geographical area and community means an abstract unity based on something other than geography. Because there are often tensions between the two types of people concerned with the two concepts, they are discussed here briefly. There can be community without neighborhood consciousness. There can also be neighborhood consciousness but little community. Those who develop community sometimes do, and sometimes do not, relate to their geographic surroundings. It seems clear, however, that much of the movement for neighborhood redevelopment, as opposed to neighborhood defense and protection, is initiated by younger residents who have a different value system from that of many of the older residents.

Some of this younger generation are what has been popularly dubbed the "counter-culture." Imbued with a sense of outrage at society's shortcomings and a consequent sense of militancy, this group has produced changes in society far outstripping their few numbers. It has been, and is, this group in particular, although with an assist from their more professional counterparts, which in large measure produces the spark that begins the reactivization of the neighborhood spirit.

The tensions are created when these people first enter a neighborhood. The counter-culture is usually the vanguard. They open the door to their more wealthy comrades. The process has been duplicated in many parts of the country, from Roxbury to Berkeley, to Washington, D.C. It works this way: Many people who want to create a new society and new ways of living want to live in group arrangements not only for the collective spirit involved, but also because they can lower living expenses to a point where they need not tie themselves to full employment to survive. This permits them time for experimentation, and travel, and private pursuits. These communal or group houses are invariably found in the lower-rent sections of town. Go into any city and you will find the counter-culture on the edge of the ghetto. Partially this is a result of their desire to live as cheaply as possible. Partially it is a result of the poor areas of the city not having the political or economic clout to keep them out. Upper-class sections do not need groups which might, in fact, lower land values instead of raising them, which, as we shall see, occurs in lower-income areas. Also, upper-class areas can demand that housing inspectors investigate group-living arrangements, can demand that housing codes be strictly enforced. The famous case of Belle Harbor, a small town on Long Island, went to the Supreme Court where the justices upheld the right of the town to prohibit unrelated individuals from living in the same house.

These groups, of five to ten people, even while earning little money, can pay more rent collectively than can a single family. So, as they move in, the rents tend to rise throughout the area. If the area they have moved into is an old section of town, or a black section of town, the presence of white people or young people on the streets changes the character of that neighborhood. Institutions such as head shops, bookstores, health-food stores, are established to cater to the new group. The "spirit" of the area changes, and then the young professionals move in, buying property, converting single family dwellings into apartment houses, and stabilizing the area in question. This process is called a "transitionary" one in real-estate lingo.

Such incursion brings with it a spurt of activity. The young are ideological, militant, and not burdened with the traditional responsibilities such as children or aged dependents, ill health, and so on.

As they set out to change their world, they typically have begun, not with a geographical focus, but with an ideological, social and cultural one. They try to find others with their brand of politics, their customs, their culture. One of the first "institutions" this group establishes in almost every city has been a switchboard — a telephone hot line that one can dial to find a ride out of town, a chess-game partner, a house to crash in for a few days. Ironically, this first institution, although having a neighborhood base, is created in order to expedite people's movement out of the neighborhood or into it only on a temporary basis. Women's groups, "rap" centers, political organizations, are the first buds of ideological community. At this early state in development only a few people are involved and there is rarely an active sense of neighborhood (the women's group meets to discuss the general topic of women's liberation, not the specific question of what to do about being approached by neighborhood males on the street). In fact we might say that geographical consciousness is inimical to the ideological, racial, or sexual consciousness that occurs at this time. Geographic consciousness tends to subordinate internal differences under the common banner of turf, while the other forms of consciousness usually accentuate differences as each person undergoes his own period of self-examination and external arrogance and stridency.

These people tend to be interested in national and international politics. Their actions in the neighborhood reflect their concern with events taking place far away. In the beginning, for example, they will support the grape pickers or they will boycott a supermarket and set up a picket line. Later, as food co-ops begin to compete with the offending supermarket, this boycott can become more effective by involving people previously disinterested in the dispute. When political principles are backed up by solid, sensible practices (such as offering cheaper, more nutritional food), people generally are more receptive to them.

The global perspective is important, and is later integrated into the total vision of the neighborhood of the future. In the same manner the concerns of the more settled residents — crime, or trash — are integrated with the political concerns of those interested in creating new work roles and social relationships, and these, in turn, are mixed with the international perspective of the highly political counter-culture. In time, the new entrants put down roots, buy houses, bear children, and the neighborhood begins to relate to the new institutions as concrete mechanisms for dealing with many of their traditional problems. The uninvolved — at first curious, and then enthusiastic — get involved and swell the numbers of those who are beginning to view the neighborhood as something special, not just a subunit of a subunit of a political system, not just a place to hang one's hat and walk one's dog, but as an independent entity, with its own hopes and aspirations and plans. A synthesis of different opinions and attitudes emerges, relying heavily on the experience that has gone before. Information from other neighborhoods and cities filters in. Communication links are established, first on a haphazard basis (passers-through bring news of new developments), then in a more formal network (WATS lines, newsletters, labor exchanges), and ideology and rootedness mix together to produce a new concept of neighborhood and territory and politics.

Information and the Breaking Down of Barriers

News in this country no longer relates to significant human concerns. The news media are controlled by a very small group of people who use the newspaper or radio or television as a vehicle for selling advertising space, not for relating to people's concerns and problems. As Ben Bagdikian, a researcher for the Brookings Institution, has written, "For all practical purposes, 'the audience' for the news media today is first a collection of people with money to spend, and only second a specific collection of citizens with private and public problems to solve." The concentration of ownership of our news sources is staggering. In 1910 there were 1,200 cities in the United States with daily papers and 57 percent had at least two. In 1970 almost 1,600 cities had daily papers but only three percent had competing managements. Bagdikian notes:

> Given the tendency for one-man direction of newspaper enterprises, at least in theory American newspaper readers have their daily printed news and opinion determined by fewer than 1,700 men, including one in each of the 1,545 cities that have only one newspaper management. Chains increase this informational centralization: 63 percent of all daily newspaper readers — members of 39.5 million households — theoretically have their printed diet controlled by 35 chains, or, possibly, 35 men.

The mass media cater to a large market, and as such cannot concern themselves with neighborhood news. It is ridiculous to think that CBS is interested in whether your landlord has given you an eviction notice, or that *The New York Times* is going to cover the opening of a local food store. We don't expect them to. But as a result we have a surplus of data and information about events mostly unconnected with our basic lives and concerns and almost no information about our neighbors, our streets, or our neighborhood.

In most city neighborhoods there is a lack of information about the area, and about one's neighbors. Rarely do people know the people living on either side of their house, or people who live on another floor of an apartment complex. If there is contact, it is on the most superficial level — perhaps only an exchange of greetings in the morning or evening. In addition, there is little knowledge about neighborhood events or basic information about the future development of the area. If there is a local baseball team, usually word gets around by mouth that they are playing in a local park on Sunday. A dance or a picnic or a church bazaar, once again, are usually known by those in and around the institutional circles. Although the person living next to you might be a master plumber, you look in the yellow pages when your sink clogs up. Even though the person down the street has a woodworking shop in his basement, you never get those shelves built because you don't have a vise or a saw.

On a different level, residents rarely know who owns their neighborhood. Does one corporation own most of the commercial property? Has land changed hands over the past year or two, indicating that speculators are moving in? What are the current sales prices of houses?

Or, on another level, what are the housing codes? What are the regulations concerning tenant unions? Can someone complain to a landlord about rats in the basement without fearing eviction?

Or, on still another level, what is the population breakdown of the neighborhood? Is it poor, rich, black, white, old, young, single, married? How many are unemployed? How many are elderly, infirm, stuck in their rooms for most of the day? How many receive welfare and food stamps?

Finally, what events looming on the horizon can affect the neighborhood? Is someone planning to build a highway through its center? Is a subway stop going to be put in the neighborhood? Is the local school or clinic closing down?

This information, and much more, is available and can provoke, for most people, the first consciousness that the neighborhood is a real entity, with definite perimeters and a definite cohesion. In fact, some of this information will be floating around the neighborhood in the form of half-truths, rumors, gossip, and fancy stories. It is important that the neighborhood learn about itself from its own inhabitants and that the information be reliable and understandable. Perhaps the most common way of doing this is through print.

Printed matter is an acceptable and familiar part of people's lives. The technology for producing it is also easily accessible and inexpensive. Offset printing, silk screening, even mimeographing, as well as conventional printing, bring the means of disseminating information to anyone. Yet it is surprising how little these tools are used in neighborhoods. Wall posters and bulletin boards on trees or telephone poles are easy ways of transmitting neighborhood news and information. Wall posters are relatively simple to design (and in the process one gets to meet the artists and photographers in the neighborhood, who inevitably become attracted to the idea of posters as information vehicles). They can be silk-screened or printed, and are colorful and easily read from a distance. Many posters on neighborhood walls, because, again, they are put there by the counter-culture, give information about upcoming rock concerts, or political demonstrations. But they can be used to relay information about the neighborhood, or to give information that might be useful for people in the area. In the Adams Morgan neighborhood of Washington, D.C., bumper stickers almost spontaneously appeared on doors and windows proclaiming "Neighbor Power," and buttons with the same slogan emblazoned jerseys and lapels.

Bulletin boards on trees invite notices (they also invite theft, so have a good supply on hand). Bulletin boards in this manner are best of all for block information, rather than neighborhood information because of the small walking radius of most residents. Examples of notices on the tree board: PHYLLIS IN 1921S STREET HAS LOST HER GREY TABBY. ANYONE SEEN IT? or PAM IN 2030 PEACH STREET JUST HAD A SEVEN-POUND BLUE-EYED BOY. SHE'S FINE AND AT HOME NOW. At first such boards may seem to be forced and artificial contrivances, but later they will be used frequently and help give a sense of something happening on that particular block.

The next step up from these bulletin boards is a neighbor-

hood newspaper. It has advantages and disadvantages. The
advantages are obvious. It provides room for exploring issues in
depth. It can be distributed in large quantities, thus getting to far
more people than those who will walk by a tree. It provides
continuity. If it comes out regularly and often, it becomes a focal
point for the community. Notices, information, articles, art work
can be sent in to the central office. People can drop by to talk. It
becomes a symbol of the embryonic community. The *Soho Times*
(New York City) or *The Columbian* (Washington, D.C.) or the
Dupont Advocate (Washington, D.C.) are all examples of such
newspapers. In addition, the newspaper can become a public
voice for the community. By having editorials and letters to the
editor, it can begin to represent the community in zoning
hearings, before the city, and in other sorts of affairs. Also a
newspaper, unlike a poster on a tree, is an individual item. Thus
information on recent land sales, on neighborhood groups, on
local important telephone numbers, can be individually saved for
future reference.

Often those who call their newspapers "community papers"
define that community as we did above, that is, as a community
of shared values rather than a specific geographic area. The *Great
Speckled Bird*, the *Austin Rag*, the *Bay Guardian* are all geared to a
specific ideological group. Their community extends far beyond
the border of the neighborhood where they are published. And, in
fact, the papers have little information that will be of interest to
the neighborhood itself. There are articles on Vietnam, on local
drug prices, on a crackdown on hippies, on protests in Chile.
There is nothing wrong with these papers. They are refreshing
examples of new journalism. They, however, serve a different
purpose from that of a neighborhood paper.

On the other hand, there are community papers which are
bland, not very informative about political issues that affect that
area, and cater to the landed gentry in the area. The *Montgomery
Advertiser*, the *Uptown Citizen*, are examples in Washington, D.C.
They do provide information about local events, carry advertise-
ments from local merchants, and have information about the
history of the neighborhood, sometimes about land transfer, and
stories about the local sports teams. They are much more oriented

toward the neighborhood, and often are a wealth of information about goings-on between the neighborhood and the city. Since the publishers and readers are the more wealthy landowners, they are the first to know of any events that might affect their land values — a proposed highway, a planned new office building, a zoning hearing.

There could be, although we do not know of one, a combination of the two described above. It would have local information about births and deaths and land transfers and picnics, but it would also have a political awareness that transcends the neighborhood scene; that is, it would have a vision of what a reconstructed neighborhood might look like and would try to educate as well as inform. This kind of paper might carry stories about other neighborhoods in the city and around the country and what they are doing, about neighborhood groups that have been organizing in various areas, about new alternative businesses. It might have a column to help people fix their cars, a classified-ad page for trade and swap, articles on people interested in forming cooperative garages. This kind of newspaper might be very difficult to carry on. It tries to blend the mundane events of the area with the lofty ideals foreseen for the new neighborhood. It could become a catalyst for getting groups together to discuss new ideas. In city after city a series of articles about one thing or another has led to the formation of study and discussion groups who then form concrete institutions. There would be problems, of course, because of the very nature of such a paper. In all probability it would have to rely on volunteer labor — at least until it had proved itself and gained a following. This might in turn mean that issues would be published irregularly and thus the paper could not be looked to for timely information. Also, volunteers may mean poorly researched articles and more interest in journalism than in the neighborhood. It may prove difficult to balance such announcements as births or deaths with news of city events or international politics. Since space will probably be limited because of cost, the question will often arise, "Should we put the story in about the local baseball game, or the one about what the neighborhoods in Berkeley are doing?"

The major initial decisions, of course, would be: How

should the paper be funded? How often should it come out? What should it look like?

Funding can come from various sources. Subscriptions are possible, although, judging from experience, quite unlikely as a primary support. The paper can be distributed free and supported by its advertisers. This, however, leads to another problem. Local merchants rarely can fully finance a paper, unless its production costs are very cheap indeed. Thus one might consider national advertising, but as soon as that happens, the problem becomes one of having to increase circulation far beyond the neighborhood in order to attract such advertisers, and having to put things in the paper which wouldn't ordinarily be thought important. Possible national advertisers might be the record companies. Locally the movie theatres are a good source of revenue. But this means reviewing records and movies, and plays and books, and little by little the paper would begin to change its format and its direction.

A paper can find donations, often from churches, in the form of free use of telephones and office space and printing press. This might be especially welcome in the beginning, when the problems of defining the paper, formulating its layout and writing the stories are so formidable that to take on fund-raising at the same time might be unwise. As one would expect, however, when relying on the largesse of any institution, there will be strings attached to that relationship. Depending on the church or group donating the money or equipment, the strings might be few or many. And almost inevitably there will be pressure for the paper to be as bland as possible, not controversial.

In Baltimore, a group of people put out the *South Baltimore Voice*, oriented toward the white working-class neighborhood in which they lived. It came out every two to three weeks, had pictures of local residents, stories about local events, and was written in a style suitable to its readership. Every month or so the workers on the paper went around with a cup to residents, asking them if they would donate to support the paper. They not only had no trouble getting enough money to pay for printing and paper and overhead, but this process also permitted them to get to know the neighborhood's problems even better, and provided a unique feedback mechanism for the readership.

How often a paper is issued tends to be a critical question. A weekly publication can provide a focal point for the neighborhood and give people a sense of continuity in local affairs. A monthly publication provides little of this symbolic cohesion for the neighborhood. It is still a good idea to have, but the difficulty with a monthly is that there will be an assumption that it will cover stories in depth the way a weekly or biweekly won't, and if the paper uses mainly volunteer labor, this is usually not true. Also, and this is crucial, the paper in the beginning, and probably for a very long time, will be most important and most read because of its classified sections — its job listings, its current events, recreation activities, and buy-sell sections. If it is a monthly, these sections cannot possibly have validity for people. A biweekly would be better; a weekly much better. In fact, experience in various cities has shown that the change from a biweekly to a weekly brings a virtual explosion of neighborhood interest in the paper. Suddenly it becomes a part of everyday life. If it comes out on a Thursday many people will read it over the weekend, and by then it is only a few days until it is published again. The classifieds and current-events sections are valid, the letters to the editor can provide almost instant feedback from the neighborhood.

Of course there are trade-offs. Publishing weekly issues is almost impossible unless there is a full-time staff. And a full-time staff raises again the question of money. Free distribution, paid subscriptions, national advertising, paid classifieds — which route to go? The choice may be to print small weekly papers or more substantial biweeklies. Consistency in publication is important, but so is content. These matters will have to be decided by each group in their own neighborhood, and based on the existing circumstances of both the group and the neighborhood. The size of staff, the amount of money, the population of the neighborhood, the presence or absence of other local publications, are all factors to be considered in arriving at decisions.

Just a few words about layout, which is important in getting and keeping people's attention. Some very general guidelines that can safely be put forth are that people tend to read shorter pieces rather than longer ones, cartoons rather than print, larger print rather than smaller, articles with pictures rather than those without. For appearance, it may be preferable to sacrifice a few inches of print than to cram a page full of words. The "hip" headlines, four-letter words and orgiastic drawings of the early "undergrounds" probably won't get you very far in most neighborhoods; a sedate appearance may, even if the content is radical (but sensible) in its direction.

There are communication tools beyond print, of course. Switchboards have sprung up around the country, as have hotlines and information-referral services. These are based on the telephone. In the case of youth-community switchboards, there is usually a central office which has listings of people with jobs, things for trade or sale, rides out of town, places to crash in the area. There could well be additional information such as what is playing at area movies, who is a good mechanic in the neighborhood, where one can find a bridge or chess player. Other types of telephone communication/information have spread in recent years. There are advertised numbers to call for advice on drugs, abortion, alcoholism, prevention of suicides. Some neighborhoods have groups who daily call elderly or handicapped residents to check on their health and needs. A telephoning network is often the most effective way of notifying neighbors of important meetings, last-minute changes, and so on. Perhaps, with a little ingenuity and organization, a lot of such information could be transmitted through a neighborhood switchboard.

Recently, there has been interest in utilizing computers for many of the functions that switchboards and classified ads have played in the past. The most advanced work on this, to our knowledge, is in San Francisco under the auspices of Resource One and the Village of Arts and Design. They have a central computer, given to them because it was obsolete, and several terminals located around the city (one in a public library, one in the Whole Earth Access Store, one in a local record store). People can use the typewriter terminal to ask questions of the computer and get answers. By typing in the word "Enter" one can put in information and by typing the word "Find" one can get information out. It is called the Community Memory System, but functions at this time rather like an electronic bulletin board. People can search out rides, things for sale (Find: Cars), and so forth. But they are beginning to explore different directions for this kind of system. Resource One obtained several computer tapes from the city which have on them basic municipal information about housing ownership, tax rates, etc. Neighborhood groups might, for example, come in and get a printout indicating which houses or apartment buildings in the city are owned by a certain landlord or corporation, or what the real-estate patterns have been in a given area of the city over the past few years, or how many housing violations a landlord has in his entire holdings. In addition, the system can easily be used to locate individuals. Find: Chess Players. Find: Windmill Experts. Find: Baseball Players. It is still embryonic, and, of course, is limited by the number of still-expensive terminals that are in operation. The amount of information the computer can carry, however, is far in excess of what newspapers can carry, and we might see the day when the computer carries most of the basic data and acts as a sort of library and clearing house for information about neighborhood reconstruction while the newspaper provides the symbolic cohesion and familiarity that we have grown accustomed to, as well as an outlet for the artists, writers, and photographers in the neighborhood.

The First Institutions: The Service Sector

The proliferation of wall posters and tree bulletin boards, the publication of a community newspaper, the beginning of familiarity with the neighborhood's basic ownership structure, permit the exchange of information about neighborhood problems. This interaction leads to the creation of the first institutions. Once again, these are often begun by those who have the free time to do so, who live in communal arrangements, and who can volunteer their help. But this is increasingly not the case. Hot-lunch programs have for a long time been the province of local churches. Day-care centers are no longer the furtive basement operations of counter-culture organizations. Free clinics have now been replaced in part by city institutions which have incorporated some of the personnel and the attitudes of these institutions.

The communication vehicles permit personal interactions and community publicity which bring together the people with problems and the people with solutions; bring together people who previously had no organization for getting together. For instance, schools have by their nature a group of people called parents whose children either do or will attend the school. Parents' associations bring these people together to discuss school questions. But there is no such association to bring together people interested in starting an abortion-counseling clinic, or a day-care center, or garden plots in the neighborhood. In order to start these, people must first know about common problems. On any given block there might be twenty mothers with two children each who are in need of a day-care center. Groups have sprung up recently based on the principle of shared-work schedules. Each parent takes one morning or afternoon a week tending the children, and pays a small overhead to cover play space, toys, and maybe trained personnel. Day-care centers have their own dynamic — they begin to discuss questions of child psychology and training, the place of sexual roles in our society, and the need for intellectual versus manual, or emotional versus intellectual, training, and at what age.

Preschool children are not the only ones in need of a new institution. Alternative elementary schools will probably spring up, and alternative high schools too. As the bureaucratic and centralized and almost fossilized educational institutions in our urban areas decay, two strong movements arise. One is toward decentralizing control over schools, the community-control movement which is perhaps strongest in parts of New York City. The other is the creation of alternative institutions, free schools, or private schools, or some arrangement in which parents or other interested persons try to create a totally new kind of learning environment. Often these new schools focus more strongly on the neighborhood, using its facilities and talents and resources for educating the children. A trip to a local watchmaker's shop, a morning's activities on a neighborhood garden, a poster contest for a neighborhood flag — all such activities permit the children to feel part of an ongoing process while giving them solid educational background.

Another area in which to get involved is in food buying. Buying clubs are now common in many cities around the country. A group of people orders food a week in advance, paying in advance, and then is able to buy in bulk. The savings are quite significant. It takes one or two part-time people, a means of transporting the bulk items, and a number of consumers who are willing to give a few hours a month in return for the benefits of good-quality, low-priced food. After a short period the routine becomes simplified. Lists of items are circulated among buying clubs in every block (or every apartment house, or every commune). Orders are brought into a central point, usually the basement of a church, although in downtown New York City this is done in people's living rooms. The produce is distributed from these same points. If for some reason there were not enough people to fill a bulk order, money is returned to the buyers. It is often difficult for buying clubs, which lack refrigeration equipment, to stock fresh produce and meat, although fresh produce in season is cheap enough, but breads, grains, and canned items are easily bought in this manner. The markup on wholesale might be a few percent in order to cover overhead like gas, one or two part-time people, and some office equipment. Even on a small-scale basis, buying clubs have been known to do thousands of dollars in business each week and to serve the needs of hundreds of families.

Health is another area which has become so expensive and isolated from people's real needs that it is vulnerable to small groups organizing to deliver good quality service on a personal level. Our medical profession rarely learns or teaches preventive medicine, only curative, and that relies on very expensive capital equipment and drug therapy which people can scarcely afford. Doctors in certain areas of the country have become so scarce that people now use emergency rooms in hospitals as regular treatment facilities. Yet emergency rooms have retaliated by charging $15 to $20 when one walks in the door, and, being located in hospitals, rely on very expensive X-ray and analysis techniques to make up for the only partially trained medical personnel (fourth-year medical students, for instance) who often staff the emergency wards.

Free clinics are one option open to people. They can concentrate on those services usually ignored by traditional medicine, and can revive the old concept of the physician being a friend as well as an expert. We are most dependent upon outside experts when we are ignorant — and we are probably most ignorant about our own bodies. Even our cars are more open to common-sense knowledge than our bodies. There are very few institutions in our communities where individuals can learn about contraception, for example, or nutrition, or abortion techniques, or signs of cancer or VD. There are very few places where one can talk out basic psychiatric problems or personal hangups. There are very few places where one can get a blood sample or urine specimen analyzed without having to answer embarrassing questions or pay an enormous amount of money. In many parts of the country, physicians are legally required to report each diagnosed case of venereal disease, which leads to inquiries about sexual partners and habits. And in some states if you are under a certain age, your parents must be notified as well. In almost no states are there facilities to treat the psychological as well as physical wounds of women who are raped (that is usually merely a police question, with policemen and women asking such pointed but ridiculous questions as "Did he penetrate?"). There are fewer, if any, places where one can go informally just to ask medical questions; these days, it requires an appointment three weeks in advance, a trip downtown, and a fee of at least $15.

The problem with free clinics, of course, is that they are parasitical if they use volunteer doctors. In any area where there is a shortage of doctors, the possibility of opening up a free medical facility is remote. It is possible, however, to have a lab clinic that does several kinds of basic analyses which require in most cases little more in the way of expensive equipment than a microscope and a centrifuge, and maybe only one trained nurse or technician plus some other non-medical staff. Another possibility, and a reality in parts of rural West Virginia and probably elsewhere, is to have "barefoot doctors" — paraprofessionals who go door-to-door, seeking out problems, giving some basic information, and prescribing non-prescription drugs or vitamins. Keep in mind that most doctors agree that ninety percent of their office visitors have either no illness at all or an uncomplicated ailment which will pass within seventy-two hours. There is almost nothing they can do for these people, except prescribe painkillers and provide assurance that the sickness is not serious. Surely such service could be administered by less than fully trained M.D.'s.

As the first institutions and communications systems develop, a neighborhood begins to have hope, to contemplate the possibilities. At this stage, maybe a small number of area residents will begin to be involved along with the counter-culture community in developing new values and meeting old needs. People will begin to have confidence that these new ways are reliable and helpful. It is at this stage, as the buying clubs are solidified, the free clinics open, the day-care centers proliferate, and the newspaper's circulation increases, that the next, and more long-lasting stage can be initiated, that of controlling increasing parts of the neighborhood's commerce, and establishing new productive facilities to meet the needs of residents.

Neighborhood Organizing

No chapter on the initial stages of neighborhood development would be complete without a discussion of the role of organizers. Essentially, this book does not concern itself with the traditional organizing concept which gathers people together to confront the centers of power to redress group grievances. Our goal in this volume is primarily concerned with ways of organizing people to create new institutions which can create the seeds of future society within the present one.

However, the two processes overlap. An organizer's skills are needed even though the goal is somewhat different. Also, as the neighborhood begins to develop strong supporting structures and moves to control or recapture its own resources, its relationship to the centers of power, both political and economic, changes. As the neighborhood begins to pull away from the underdeveloped-nation status to one of self-rule, larger interests may begin to feel threatened by the possibility of this tendency being duplicated in other underdeveloped parts of the country. (Still, by the time this occurs an organizer's skills may no longer be the necessary ones, for the neighborhood itself, through its newly developed institutions and productive facilities, will respond through its own political institutions to pressure from external bodies.)

The literature on organizing and organizers is, surprisingly, very scant. Most books and articles are descriptive and deal with political organizing, that is, the development of vehicles for gaining elective political office. Although there is a small, but growing body of literature on organizing around consumer issues, most of this is directed at either individual action or legislative goals, not community-building.

In the material which is available one primary lesson stands out — there are few strict rules or strategies for the organizer. Si Kahn, a long time organizer in the rural south, said, "If I have learned anything . . . it is that there are really no rules for organizers — only experiences." Saul Alinsky, the premier urban organizer, put it this way: "People ask me, 'Say, you're going to organize the middle class? How are you going to start?' All I know is what every really good organizer knows — you react to all the action with a reflex: 'How do I use this to build the organization?' "

After giving this caveat, all the organizers invariably go on to write long treatises on how-to aspects of organizing, indicating that even though they emphasize the play-it-by-ear approach, there are some things that neophytes might consider important, insights gained from their experiences in the field. Perhaps the most important insight is that organizers must start where the people are and work through the self-interest of those people. Appeals to lofty sentiment and morality will not work in most cases, and will attract only intermittent attention in others. Here again there is a difference between those who feel part of a community of shared values, and those who feel part of a geographically based neighborhood. Often those in the community, particularly the political young, will respond to a call to conscience and participate in activities even when their own self-interest is not involved. The resistance to the Vietnam War provided countless examples of this. Conscience can be a strong motivating factor, but it is also true that the Vietnam War taught us that there is little staying power derived from using morality as the driving force. It often produces orgasmic responses — spontaneous actions and decisions which last for a short time. There is a concrete reason for this. The lofty ideals of conscience confront the mundane bureaucratic regulations of the state. The confrontations with police over the Vietnam War are vivid memories. We were there to struggle with the military over the question of wanton destruction of an entire nation, and yet the real struggle, that is the basic decision as to whether we wanted to be hit over the head or go to jail, usually centered on obscure regulations and ordinances. Did we have a permit to march? Were we stepping off the sidewalk? Were we standing still when we should have been moving? The frustration of trying to combat a heinous crime while going to jail over such minor regulations led people to dramatically and publicly do other things, like pouring blood over draft files, to make themselves moral witnesses, to make individual statements while forsaking sustained effort at building ongoing institutional structures.

Every organizer repeats the refrain, "Start where people are." Put any kind of program you might have within people's own frame of reference, appealing to their own self-interest. As Alinsky put it: "In a mass organization, you can't go outside of people's actual experience." David Lilienthal, former head of the T.V.A., makes the point with this anecdote:

> We move step-by-step from where we are. Everyone has heard the story of the man who was asked by a stranger how he could get to Jonesville. After long thought and unsuccessful attempts to explain the several turns that must be made, he said, so the anecdote runs, "My friend, I tell you; if I were you, I wouldn't start from here."

Many times we do not want to "start from here." We would like to start with a clean slate, a willing community upon which we can imprint our ways of thinking. But this is impossible. Every neighborhood has its own traditions, its own prejudices, and its own conventional wisdom. The first task of an organizer is, in fact, to discover what the neighborhood is, and this is done not by proclaiming programs, but by listening. "Actually," notes Alinsky, "you do more organizing with your ears than with your tongue." Listening helps to discover not only the customs of the neighborhood, but what its residents believe its problems to be, who the natural leaders are, and what the history of struggle and organization has been in that area.

Although it might be self-evident, the first thing one can do by listening is to discover what the perimeters of the neighborhood are. As Milton Kotler notes:

> The most sensible way to locate the neighborhood is to ask people where it is, for people spend much time fixing its boundaries. Gangs mark its turf. Old people watch for its new faces. Children figure out safe routes between home and school. People walk their dogs through their neighborhood, but rarely beyond it. Above all the neighborhood has a name: Hyde Park or Lake View in Chicago; Roxbury, Jamaica Plain or Beacon Hill in Boston.

Simultaneously with the discovery of the natural perimeters of the neighborhood the organizer can discover the natural leaders of the community. There may be many. Frequently they are not known outside the area, or even by many people inside the neighborhood, but they have a following based on respect for their wisdom, or their dedication, or their hard work. Alinsky feels that "One of the most important tasks of the organizer, in addition to identifying these natural leaders, and working with them, is working for their actual development so that they become recognized by their following as leaders in more than one limited sphere." He adds that the development of local leadership "does not mean what so many people think, that there is not leadership among the rank and file. There is leadership, but it is the partial variety, and its development is the development of partial leaders into well-rounded leaders of their people."

This question of leadership will be expanded when we discuss neighborhood government, for it is a double-edged sword. It is necessary to have those in a neighborhood who are already respected because of one trait or another begin to recognize and utilize their positions of respect to catalyze a new direction for neighborhood development. But, as more and more of their neighbors join in the movement, and add their input to its development, these natural leaders can become a brake on further development if they have in the process forsaken their real foundations of leadership — respect by their neighbors — for the symbolic kind of leadership which comes from elected office, rank, or municipal publicity and recognition.

Gaining a knowledge of the needs of the neighborhood means, once again, working from where people are, not where we would like them to be. It is irrelevant to speak to people about free clinics if their major concern is an urban-renewal project or a new highway going through the middle of their territory.

We should emphasize here that acting in a manner which is consistent with people's traditions does not mean stagnating, or moving slowly, or lacking imagination. This is very important. Those who are assisting in the first stages of neighborhood development must have a vision, even a program, for the future. They may want to transform the neighborhood in which they live into a developed country, with political institutions based on participation, not representation, democracy extended to every level, including the schools, the hospitals, the businesses, and the family. They may want just compensation for labor and community control over turf and its resources. They may want the neighborhood to control the surplus capital it generates, and may desire a cooperative society based on trust and mutual assistance. Without a fairly concrete vision there is nothing to motivate future actions, nothing to measure success against, and no way to evaluate new turns and twists in the original program.

Still, the vision should be one that the residents can understand. Pushing for vague and threatening programs like "building the socialist state," or "anarchy," or "collectivization of property," or "overthrowing the ruling class" leads to little progress in meeting people's real needs. There are major groups in this country who honestly believe that it doesn't matter if there is any substantial progress toward meeting people's real needs; they feel that the basic need is for people to be educated and made aware of the class structure of this society, that people need to be given a context and perspective in which to place all the actions they see and read about. Thus workers, under this theory, must be convinced of their class oppression and power, even if initially the words that describe this turn off large segments of that very "class." The reasoning behind this theory is simple: the ruling elite cannot permit any significant opposition among those who are in positions of leverage in the society (e.g., workers). Therefore they will jail, harass, kill, or fire those who begin to move in that direction. Without a class analysis or context those who are oppressed will be confused, not able to place the growing repressive acts of the ruling class in any context. With such an understanding, these acts become cumulative, mounting on an individual's consciousness until an explosion ensues. Revolution bursts on the scene with widespread violence, general strikes, and armed struggle. Only when that occurs is there the possibility of success against the armed might of the state. So the theory goes.

The theory is attractive, although probably more so because it permits most people to avoid doing hard work on the local level while they try to refine their rhetoric and ideas until they achieve the final "correct" position. But in a more basic sense it's wrong-headed because it does not relate to people where they are, and particularly does not do so through an optimistic vision of the future. The sectarianism of the left is often caused by too much talking and too little doing. Picky fights about dogma tend to subside as people work together in some productive enterprise. Or at least the arguments are over very real things. What should be done when a worker breaks a leg and the company refuses compensation is a question that lends itself to much more concrete analysis than what should be done when the workers take over the factory and the army comes in.

What is not as obvious, yet even more important, is that only through attracting people to a vision of how things can be different can they enter the long period of change with optimism and joy and camaraderie. Most analyses of what needs to be done are grim, pessimistic, even fatalistic. In our activities in neighborhoods and communities we have now come to the point where we can divide people not into radicals and conservatives, but into pessimists and optimists. Community residents catch on pretty quick that this revolutionary talk is all a game, that the armed might of the state is too strong, that the only thing you can do is be the first one on your block killed at the barricades. But when residents' real needs are being met by people in their community, then a dialogue is opened up that grows and becomes more and more attractive.

A concrete example of this occurred in our own efforts in Adams Morgan. When we speak of government oppression or immorality, we speak to people who intuitively know that already, but who are also accepting of the conventional wisdom that big government and big business, for all their inefficiency and corruption, are necessary to produce the good life of abundance that we all have a little piece of. But when we speak of food co-ops, or raising trout in basements or vegetables on rooftops, or community manufacturing facilities, we move out of the ideological realm and present a vision that everyone can participate in. Both authors have anecdotal experiences about this: David Morris was speaking for the second time on the Barry Farber Show in New York. The first time he spoke on the revolutionary process in Chile. The second time he spoke about neighborhood food systems. When he ended his second talk, Farber noted over the air that the "first time we talked we had disagreements about politics, but no one could disagree with the sort of thing he is doing now." In another instance James J. Kilpatrick, conservative commentator, debated Karl Hess in Clemson, South Carolina, on the topic "Which Way America: Left or Right?" Kilpatrick later wrote about the debate: "He was speaking for the New Left, I for the Old Right, but before the evening was over we were talking about fish in his basement and tomatoes on his roof." Left and Right labels disappear when people's real needs and creativity are taken into account. Rhetorical flourishes concerning private property, or sexism, or capitalism or racism, must become much more concrete when they are put in the context of neighborhood events. Maybe the new motto should be, "Think Small to Produce Big Changes."

As we said before, even though people cannot be pushed into new positions too fast, neighbors who want to move in new directions should know where they want to go. They should know how tenant unions, food co-ops, vegetable raising, neighborhood government, political demonstrations, are all part of an integrated and revitalized neighborhood. A good way to do this is to present the information graphically. In Washington, D.C., in early 1968, at the peak of the anti-war movement and the eve of its greatest triumph, McCarthy's victory in New Hampshire, a tiny group of people came together to proclaim the birth of the Washington Free Community. Nothing existed at the time except a community newspaper and three or four communal living arrangements. But there had been murmurings of new institutions and we thought it important to outline where we hoped these new events might carry us.

The publication of the chart caused no sensation. It was premature. The community and the neighborhood were not yet ready for it. But it helped to get the idea in front of people. Others in the country were talking about Woodstock Nation, or the third-world community. Ours was a different vision, and carried a basically different message. The name Washington Free Community stuck for three years, defining a counter-culture community of shared value. Interestingly, as the institutions' outlines in the chart developed and grew, the name changed to Alternate Economy, indicating that there still was a shared value system but that now it was based on more sophisticated concepts of economics and production and income distribution, rather than cultural events and concepts. Simultaneously the neighborhood concept and name, Adams Morgan, began to compete in people's consciousness with the community name, and the interaction of community and neighborhood, with its inherent tensions and potentials, began.

A vision is important, although perhaps not crucial. It helps people to know where they are going, and it perhaps helps answer the question, why. In some cities, for example, some of the food cooperatives, although very large and influential, have not seen themselves as part of a developing community and therefore have become consumer cooperatives, avoiding or ignoring the questions of surplus capital and their role in the creation of community-owned manufacturing facilities. In Chicago the Citizens Action Project (CAP) has a clear vision of itself as a coalition of neighborhood and city groups which struggle against the city bureaucracy, with the goal, according to one of its founders, of eventually becoming one of the fibers of a national mass party. Such a divergence of vision helps to produce reaction, participation, and development, whereas vague programs and plans lead to chaotic development that may or may not work out.

The vision psychologically helps in giving a lift to people participating in various activities. Many different people, whether they are assisting the elderly to get hot lunches, or initiating a community-sustaining fund, or starting a wind-energy group, or a tenant union, can feel part of a common effort with a fairly common goal. Since the struggle is a hard and long one and there is precious little compensation except for mutual assistance and satisfaction and psychological lift from the togetherness of struggle, this becomes a very important safety valve against "burning out" after a time and moving back into regular jobs in city bureaucracies or private industry. A coherent vision provides this safety valve.

THREE

Controlling the Local Economy:
The Growth of
Community Businesses

When the first alternative service organizations were begun, their internal structure was not an immediate problem. There was a great deal of enthusiasm and volunteer labor, and very little money (usually from foundation grants). The service was the important thing, whether it was in free clinics, buying clubs, switchboards, or political organizations. Since there was no compensation adequate to make the job attractive to entrepreneurs, no prestige inherent in the work, and no use of such jobs as stepping stones to higher employment, only a certain type of person joined. Sometimes it was the dedicated youth working for $25 to $50 a week. Occasionally, professional people volunteered their services a few hours a week.

The primary question in these new organizations was how to relate in a better way to the "consumer" — how to transform the traditional dependency relationship, with one person buying another's skills, to one of two-way interaction, with people helping each other to help themselves. In many cases this meant demystifying the special and esoteric words and actions of the traditional service sector, teaching people not to be afraid of involving themselves in their own medical problems, or legal disputes, or child care. Since the consumers often did not pay for

46

the services (although occasionally there were contributions requested), the marketplace only vaguely played a role in determining the quality of the services.

However, volunteer labor, foundation grants, $25-a-week salaries, are flimsy foundations for a new society. At some time in a neighborhood's development, the large flow of capital within the local economy has to be tapped. This flow is often substantial, even in poor neighborhoods. As Milton Kotler has written:

> The important features of a poor neighborhood are, first, the discrepancy between the aggregate expendable income of the neighborhood and the paltry level of its commerce, and, second, the discrepancy between the considerable tax revenue the neighborhood generates and the low level of benefits it receives in public services and welfare. In both cases the neighborhood exports its income . . . . Its present internal commerce is dependent, as is its level of public services, on commerce and personnel outside the neighborhood.

The question of neighborhood taxation is discussed in the next chapter. The disparity between neighborhood aggregate income and neighborhood commerce is often striking. As a neighborhood becomes aware of this disparity, retail stores begin to operate to capture this capital. As these stores begin to spread, a different process from that of the spread of service institutions takes place. Questions of internal structure, of worker control, of surplus capital become critical. This is the stage when people relate most closely to traditional capitalist assumptions and it can be viewed as a crucial testing time for untried assumptions about the nature of our economic system. It is a time when our ideals about cooperation and mutual aid often founder because, like it or not, this system which has weaned us and educated us and supported us has also not so subtly implanted a value system which is extraordinarily difficult to exorcise. An economic system which is based on the inherent greediness and evil of human beings breeds suspicion, distrust, inequality, and armed might. Big government, it is taught, is established to protect those with money against the rest of us and to protect us against ourselves. Big business, it is taught, is a natural extension of open competition, and produces efficient products. Workers need supervisors if they are not to reduce production out of sheer slothfulness. Money is the ultimate incentive and it is quite efficient in keeping people in line and channeling their evil energies into socially beneficial work. Assumptions such as these, usually somewhere just below the surface, rise to the top during the period of chaos which inevitably follows initial experimentation with new ideas and concepts and structures.

Retail stores often develop from the cooperative services or buying clubs described in the last chapter. There are many good examples of this in the buying of food. For instance, in Washington, D.C., a buying club called Glut was initiated in the late 1960s. Its operations were similar to buying clubs all over the country. People would go to a central point and check off what they wanted to buy, pay the charge, and return the next week to pick up the purchases. This permitted buying of goods in large lots and therefore lower prices. Handling charges and labor and overhead costs were kept to a minimum and this contributed to the low cost of the items also.

The process attracted so many customers that it exceeded the administrative capacity of the small mostly volunteer group. The city-wide buying club was then divided into neighborhood buying associations. These worked fairly well, relying on block buying clubs that were familial in nature. But there were limitations. First, the block clubs could only involve those who could and would buy a week ahead of time. This turned out to be more people than one would imagine in this society of instant gratification, but still only a small fraction of the neighborhood's shoppers. Second, as the number of people involved even at the neighborhood level swelled, the mechanism for collecting money and distributing goods was overloaded once again. Third, if the buying club could not buy in whole lots, it had to cancel the order and return the money to the customers, inconveniencing and frustrating them. This also caused burdensome bookkeeping. Fourth, the block associations had to pool their orders, taking them to a local church basement, bringing back the goods from a warehouse and distributing them within the block. The system worked surprisingly well, and still operates, but was difficult to routinize.

When a space in the neighborhood became available, a store was rented and began to operate on a cash-and-carry basis. The opening of a regular grocery store brought with it the first step toward what might be called social realism, dealing with immediate problems of delivery systems and merchandising. The food-buying clubs, although important as organizing vehicles, educating mechanisms, and primitive delivery systems, pre-select those who buy through them, while grocery stores are open to anyone and therefore have a different job in relating to the surrounding community.

From the initial experiment with a cash-and-carry food store has come, at least in Washington, D.C., a flood of experiments with other kinds of retail stores, like record shops, flower shops, hardware stores, pharmacies. The food stores (for there are now four on the retail level) have combined into the Washington Food Federation and have started a produce and grain warehouse, a trucking collective and the beginnings of food processing plants, and have developed embryonic links with farmers in the area.

The growth of small business on the retail level, and the vertical integration between retailing, wholesaling, distribution and production are well-known phenomena in American history. The arguments against such a development are also well known: a small business can't compete with a large business and even if it could, it must then adopt many of the policies of traditional market capitalism, becoming more and more like the very institution it is trying to replace. These arguments are quite valid and pointed. They should be kept in mind whenever attempting to give perspective to the entire alternate-economy idea. It is also true, however, that no talk about reform, or revolution, or structural change, can be meaningful unless it concerns concrete mechanisms for the production and delivery of goods and services. It is always easier to say we need to change everything before we change anything, that everything is so interrelated that to pick off a piece of it is to be tied in frustration and indeed, thereby to be counterproductive, failing, and, in that failure, proving that any different kind of economic arrangement is unworkable. An excellent case can be made in support of this argument. Small stores depend on wholesalers. Wholesalers depend on processing plants and manufacturers. Very large corporations get tax breaks and subsidies at almost every step along the way. The link between the large corporations and the financial sector makes it easier for them to get finance capital. The relationship between big business and big government makes it easier for them to get favorable legislation passed. The laws of this country were not ever written to support low prices, or non-profit businesses, or community-oriented institutions.

Yet having admitted all this, it is also true that the very large institutions have become so bureaucratic and so dependent on outside subsidies and so large that they have also become impersonal, uncreative, and, in the final analysis, *inefficient* in the production and delivery of goods and services. This inefficiency is sometimes reflected in price; it is always reflected in quality of service and in other intangible ways. It is those intangibles which comprise a good deal of the educational program of the new community businesses. A food supermarket such as Safeway makes some of its profits through the death of farmworkers in southern California, a result of the use of pesticides in the fields and the fight of Safeway and the large agri-business groups against the farmworkers' right to organize their own unions. A small Safeway store in a neighborhood in Washington, D.C., moved in after agreeing to keep the area around its store clean of refuse and debris, and promptly forgot about the agreement. In many stores hired help is paid only $2 an hour and the owner lives outside the area, gaining the profits without giving the labor. Concepts such as the relationship of one's labor to one's wealth, the relationship of the business to its community, the relationship of the business in the community to its other branches throughout the nation and the world, all of these become important as community businesses try to teach the neighborhood what a business could and should look like.

Conspiracies, Cooperatives, Collectives, and CDC's

Perhaps the most important question in opening a business is, "What should be its internal structure?" There are many different kinds of structures to choose from. Often people invent hybrid forms, selecting the best aspects of each type and incorporating them into a new structure. Each of the structures described below deals with the questions: What is the relationship of the workers to the management of the store? What is the relationship of the store to the neighborhood? What is the relationship of the consumers to the workers or the management?

Food conspiracies have grown during the past few years. They are usually fairly informal arrangements, operating somewhere between the buying-club stage and the cash-and-carry-store stage. They rely heavily on volunteer labor. Usually, volunteers agree to work a certain number of hours per week and in return get a discount on their groceries or purchases. A restaurant in Philadelphia operates on this basis. In the food conspiracy in Tucson, Arizona, there are two levels. Those people who volunteer their labor get a 15 percent discount on food. Those who don't volunteer their labor pay the full price, which may be just a little over what it would be in a supermarket. The volunteering of labor avoids many of the questions about worker relationship with management and is thought to be helpful in building cooperative community. Often sharing arrangements flow out of the initial operation, leading to other kinds of retail operations. Usually, there are a few full-time staff, who are paid subsistence salaries of $25 to $40 per week.

Cooperatives are quite an old idea in the world and in this country. Although there are both producer and consumer cooperatives, most co-ops in this country are for consumers. The basic principle underlying any co-op is that those who buy at the store own it. Each member gets one vote, independent of how much money is invested in the company.

Surplus is returned to a member who has used the store in the form of a dividend based on the amount the person has spent at the store (called a patronage fund). Co-ops are limited by law in the amount of dividends they can give to their members, with eight percent being the upper limit.

In typical cooperatives the members elect the directors at annual meetings and the directors in turn hire a manager, someone with expertise in the business. The manager hires the staff who are paid employees of the enterprise and may or may not be members of the co-op.

Conventional co-ops usually charge the regular retail price and members get discounts through a rebate at the end of the year. Members buy shares of stock in the enterprise, costing $5 to $20 per share, but no matter how many shares they buy they can only vote once. This money becomes the operating capital for the enterprise.

There are also *discount cooperatives,* a recent innovation. They work in similar fashion to the conventional co-ops except that the members are charged the wholesale purchase price plus a certain percentage. In other words, there is a markup above wholesale costs to cover overhead.

Still another kind of co-op is called the *direct-charge co-op.* This sells goods to members at wholesale cost. Each member is assessed weekly or monthly to cover the operating costs. The advantage of this situation appears to be that members can more directly know how much the co-op is costing them, for they get a separate bill each week or month rather than figuring out the markups on food.

Worker collectives typically operate as traditional cash-and-carry stores. There are no employees or employers in the traditional sense. Each person who works there is paid and is part of the board of directors. Decisions are often made by consensus. Newcomers to the collective may have to wait a trial period before gaining full membership but even during this period have full voting power. Meetings are open to the community which has a voice, but not a vote, in crucial decisions.

A *community-development corporation,* or CDC, is a corporation based in one geographic area and controlled by its residents. The most common procedure is to sell two types of shares in the corporation. Class A shares are sold to anyone, and are usually used to raise risk capital from donations, church groups, and rich patrons. The owners of these shares earn dividends much in the manner of preferred stock, but have no voting power. Class B stockholders are neighborhood residents who pay a nominal amount, perhaps $5 a share, and earn a dividend but also have a voting right. As on the co-ops, a person has one vote no matter how many shares he or she possesses. CDC's are generally profit-making ventures, although the surplus goes to the resident shareholders and employees. A typical CDC is in Durham, North Carolina, called United Durham, Inc. (UDI). It evolved from the United Organization for Community Involvement, an organization representing twenty-one different neighborhoods with populations ranging from 800 to 3,000. This organization established a series of self-help groups in the community, helped negotiate with the city to get more street lights and stop signs, helped neighborhood clean-up campaigns, and had a casual employment center for those interested in part-time or temporary work. Money was raised from a church foundation and from benefits, dances, bake sales, and speaking honoraria as the organization became well known. Superimposed on this was the UDI, having great community support.

There are many permutations and combinations of economic forms derived from the above. In Philadelphia, for example, cooperative stores have three classes of customers. There are working members, who give six hours of labor per month and in return get a fifteen percent discount on prices; there are non-working members who, like working members, pay $5 a year membership fee but do not give volunteer labor and receive a ten percent discount; and finally, there are those who are neither volunteers nor dues-paying members and who get no discount at all. In Minneapolis the cooperative food stores have let their customers decide what they want the markup to be, choosing any percentage between ten and twenty percent. (The customers' average markup turned out to be thirteen percent.)

Each of the economic structures has its advantages and disadvantages. The conventional co-ops and direct-charge co-ops have an easier time raising money for operating costs. Their problem is that they cater to a small group of people and their internal structure is hierarchical. There is a management and there are workers and, because the shareholders are the customers, the orientation favors consumer interests rather than profit, but not more democratic work relationships. Co-ops work best when they are small so that the principle of economic democracy can truly work out. But most of them grow to a very large size (did you know that Welch's grape juice and Sunkist orange juice are products of cooperatives?) and in that case they act much like any other corporation, with little membership participation or influence. Many co-ops, like the food store in Berkeley, California, have excellent merchandise and displays and fairly good prices, but do not relate to the community around them. This is probably an unfair complaint to make about co-ops because they were never initiated to help in neighborhood development but, rather, to supply high-quality goods and services at low cost for their members, and since their members do not necessarily live in the immediate vicinity of the store, there are no attachments to the neighborhood itself.

The food conspiracies are unstable and fragile because they have to rely so heavily on volunteer labor. They are more political than economic, trying to build a cooperative, socialist society rather than trying to provide widespread and consistent services while making a viable living.

The worker collectives are new arrivals on the American scene; consequently there is not as much information to draw from in evaluating them. One possible difficulty arises, however, when choices have to be made about dividing up the surplus, assuming there is a surplus. There are several alternatives. Prices can be reduced, thereby giving back to the consumers what they have been "overcharged" during the year. This is the most common practice in cooperatives and collectives. Wages can be raised among the staff. This will happen in any case because wages start off at a very low level. The question is, at what level do wages become private profits? Surplus can be used to expand the business itself or for extracurricular activities in the community (e.g., supporting political demonstrations, giving out free food or merchandise). Or the surplus can be placed in a community fund for further community development, to be allocated by vote of the community itself. Or it can go to further productive facilities within the community at large.

These are difficult questions but important ones for future development. If the neighborhood is treated as an underdeveloped nation, then it seems clear that capital must be generated from some source. Reducing prices from fifteen to twenty percent below comparable supermarket prices eliminates the possibility of having enough capital to start other such enterprises. The question of consumerism versus production must be considered in any such decision.

At the same time another question arises. Who should make these decisions? In the CDC's such a decision could be made by the holders of Class B stock. In the cooperatives, by law dividends are limited and patronage refunds are established. In conspiracies and worker collectives the newness of the institutions and their informality mean that these questions have not yet been raised. Should the workers make the final decision? The patrons of the store? Or the neighborhood itself?

No matter what the choice, there are other important decisions awaiting the business long before it has to deal with the crucial but happy question of what to do with the surplus. The first is, what role should the store play in educating the neighborhood? Co-ops, although having education as an essential part of their program, are very lax in this. Some have eliminated non-returnable bottles. Some have organic food. But few are political enough to describe corporate relationships to consumerism or why our food supply is so heavily laced with chemicals.

What will the store carry in the way of merchandise? A record co-op in Washington, D.C., decided that it would carry mainly small-company labels. A bookstore decided to carry only political books. These kinds of decisions are fairly easy to make. For a food store it is much harder. Should the store carry many varieties of breakfast cereals or none at all? One or two varieties of catsup, or mustard? It is easier to carry only one brand, since it cuts down on the amount of shelf space needed and also makes buying easier. But decisions such as these go right to the heart of whether the store is there to serve its consumers by giving them

whatever they want, or educating them about the role nutrition
plays in health and the role corporations play in product
merchandising. There is always a trade-off. In some cases, like
varieties of tunafish or catsup, it doesn't seem to matter if there
are one or two brands. Maybe that is because people have not yet
been persuaded that there is a major difference among tunafish
brands. But with other items, like white bread or breakfast
cereals, the decisions are more difficult. People not only really like
corn flakes or Kaboom, but they also are addicted to high sugar
levels and find it physically difficult to break the cycle. In this
area, perhaps the store should try to educate people slowly,
instead of laying down the law. This is partially a tactical
question. People who discover that a store doesn't carry what they
want will not shop there, especially if the store people are
heavy-handed about the harm these foods can bring. But people
can be gradually educated about alternatives. A good suggestion
is to have several articles about the lack of nutrition in white,
bleached flour, and articles about white bread and experiments
performed on rats, and then leave the white bread on the shelves
but surround it with numerous whole grain and organic breads.
Ask people if they have stopped using white bread and how they
feel. It is coercive, but only slightly, and it is educational. There
are some items that a collective might feel it cannot in good
conscience carry — like Twinkies, or soda pop — but once again
it would be practical to carry sweet substitutes, like raisins or
carob cookies, explaining to people that they are just as filling,
just as satisfying, but not as unhealthy.

Some alternative stores, for political reasons, will not carry
certain items like lettuce and grapes from farms refusing to
negotiate with the United Farmworkers. Stores should make
absolutely clear to their patrons why they are doing this.

It is crucial not to assume that people already know about
the farmworkers' struggle, or the harm that Twinkies can do, or
the relationship between the proliferation of breakfast cereals and
the plight of the small farmer. Many do not know these things.
And so long as they do not know, and perhaps even after they do
know, they will not quickly change their habits. America teaches
us above all the concepts of individualism and free choice. There

are some people, highly intelligent, who hold that the most important idea in this country is the right of people to have fifty varieties of breakfast cereals to choose from. It might be possible after six months or a year, however, for members of the collective to decide that they want to drop an item and explain to patrons why they have done this.

We have talked about the structure of the store. We will concentrate now on the worker collectives because, although there are severe limitations, we think they are going in the right direction in responding to a need to integrate work, community, and consumerism.

The primary difficulty with worker collectives is how to stop them from becoming extended "mom and pop" stores, that is, self-serving except with ten owners rather than just one. There is always a built-in mechanism for stopping capital and labor from separating, because at no time can someone put money into the store rather than work there, but that doesn't prevent the workers from putting their own interests ahead of the community. This, of course, is a problem whenever one speaks of worker control in any context.

In Washington, D.C., members of one worker collective, a food store, voted themselves a tentative five-week paid vacation. It was clear that they were a little embarrassed by this action because their weekly newsletter, which usually covered all the trivial and major decisions of the store, conspicuously left this one out. Word got around anyway and the community raised some important questions. The ensuing dialogue indicates the complexity of the problem and the fact that all sides deserve a fair hearing.

The workers explained that they were then making $100 per week, about average for retail workers around the country. A five-week paid vacation was the equivalent of having one more worker, and, if it were taken as higher pay, would come to a $20-a-week increase. Furthermore, and more to the point, by controlling their time they were demonstrating what worker collectives are all about in a manner much more dramatic than raising their own wages. Control over time is a luxury that only the highest professionals usually retain. Strong unions can get

wage increases, but only when workers *are* the management can
they control their own time.

Finally, and candidly, they made the point that working in a
grocery store was shitwork for the most part — hard, repetitive
work — forty to fifty hours a week, with little respite. If they did
not have a long vacation, many of them would "burn themselves
out" making a great effort for a while and then leaving the area to
live on a farm, take a straight job, or travel. Why, they further
asked, should professionals and teachers, who take home triple
and quadruple their salaries for far easier and more rewarding
work, also be able to take one- or two-month vacations while
retail blue-collar workers can't? Besides, they repeated, this was
not meant to be an exclusive action. Everyone was working
toward a better society where everyone would have adequate
leisure time. In their meetings about the matter they did not ask,
"How much vacation can we take?" but rather had long
discussions on how much vacation everyone in a new society
should have. They arrived at the five-week figure and wanted it
extended to as many parts of the community as feasible.

The response of some in the community was that, by taking
such a long paid vacation, the collective seemed to be saying to
the community that the process of structural change was far
enough along for some to take long vacations, and for part of the
surplus capital to be utilized in giving some people comfort over
others, when, in fact, many people believed the process was just
beginning. Also, this store had done surprisingly well. It was in a
good location, and had a good clientele and excellent publicity
because of its unique nature. Should this accidental circumstance
of having an empty building at the right time and at the right
location give them an edge over their companions in other stores?
What if other collectives did not do as well? Under traditional
capitalism the choice of location is considered part of one's
business acumen, and if one does well, one reaps the benefits of
one's wisdom. Was the same to hold true here?

Furthermore, what would happen in the community if
inequalities persisted? What hope would there be of people
rotating through the different businesses if one had something real
and material to lose by so doing? And, finally, what would be the

effect on the composition of the collective itself? With a salary of $100 per week and a five-week paid vacation, the job would suddenly become one of the most attractive semi-skilled or unskilled jobs in the country. Would not the collective begin to attract those more interested in the material benefits of the job rather than in taking part in a developing social process?

These were all very concrete questions. But perhaps the most difficult problem was that there was no mechanism available which could help work out the problems. The consumers, who were, in fact, being taxed to benefit the workers, could not directly have any influence. The incident raised the spectre of a worker collective becoming like a mom-and-pop store, out for personal gain over community benefit. The argument was put forward by some members of the collective that the price of goods in the store couldn't be lowered by more than a fraction of a penny in any case so why not help the workers who had devoted part of their lives to developing the enterprise? It's a simple, but facile argument, for it is also used to justify Henry Ford's salary, which comes to no more than a few pennies a car.

The dispute was dealt with as most will be at the early stages of neighborhood and community development, through trust and mutual confidence. It was discovered that the store had loaned out large amounts of money to start other businesses and had doubled its staff in just a few months, rather than raise individual salaries. The community felt satisfied that there was no rip-off involved. The store's members decided to reconsider their decision, and, in fact, dropped the whole idea within a few weeks.

This dispute raises questions not only about worker collectives, but about the creation of mechanisms for resolving these kinds of conflicts. At this stage of development, the neighborhood has no institutions for problem solving and there is no general assembly that might be interested in the question. It is impossible, in any case, to begin to create bureaucratic mechanisms to resolve questions such as these, because there must be a solid foundation of mutual trust to begin with; if not, the mechanisms themselves will not be used, or not be honored, or will have to become coercive in their judgments.

Although not a critical question in the beginning, the

composition of the work force in these community businesses becomes much more important in later months and years. In the beginning there are the "pioneers," who have a vision of what the store could be, who have the ego satisfaction of starting it and seeing the community respond to it, and who have a sense of movement and process. This first generation of workers, however, rarely stays long at the job. Possibly this is because of the nature of the job — hard work at low pay for long hours. Possibly it is because the people who start such projects are middle-class and have difficulty seeing themselves as grocery personnel for a long period of time. In addition, some pioneers, by their very nature, are interested in creating and establishing such institutions, not in running them after they are set up, and the success of one store sparks them to go on to other enterprises. The second generation of workers and then the third generation comes in, and they have a different situation. The beginning of the store fades into the past. Those struggles are over. The initial enthusiasm and publicity and so forth are past also. New stores have been established in other industries and they are getting more publicity than the first. Sometimes, as a result of having learned from the experiences of the first store these others are better, bigger, brighter. Because the first store was successful, the others had less difficulty raising money from local investors and community people and so they could start up much easier. Thus the second and third generations of workers find themselves in a job much like any other job except that the work conditions are vastly superior. This is a critical period in the store's history. Many new members do not have the drive of the pioneers, nor their politics. The enthusiasm for the store is not there, although they do their jobs creditably.

One possible result is that during this period of time there will be a great turnover in personnel as people wander in and out of the work force depending on personal preferences. No longer feeling part of an ongoing process, they leave a lot of the decision-making to the still-working pioneers and see the job as a relatively good one rather than an important part of neighborhood reconstruction. A high turnover of personnel can emotionally debilitate the store. It is one reason why cooperatives, with their trained managers and hired staff, can have continuity without worrying about turnover. It is one reason why volunteer food conspiracies can have a lot of excitement for a long time, because there are new faces coming in, the work is not full-time, and there is a continuity of enthusiasm and work force.

There are several ways to overcome this inevitable problem. One is to rotate personnel throughout the federation of community businesses in order to give each worker a concrete sense of what he or she is part of, as well as changing the surroundings and the friendship groups. This, however, is very difficult because it might be a long time before there are enough community businesses to warrant such a rotation. Rotating jobs puts a strain on each collective for each must then initiate new, untrained personnel into work schedules fairly often. Another, and more immediate solution is to select the personnel very carefully. Each worker collective should probably have a balance of personnel. For example, there could be some who are pioneers, who are entrepreneurial, have a vision far beyond the one store, and can be expected to work on those other projects for part of their time, becoming a sort of cog that holds different institutions together. There could also be some who are devoted to the store itself but who see it primarily as an educational and political vehicle. These people will raise questions of equity and community involvement at meetings, will put out the community newsletters which are the prime contact point with the community, will put literature throughout the store which is useful for consumers, and will demand that non-union lettuce and Chilean wines not be carried in the store. And, finally, there could be people who see the store as a business, who want it to be financially sound, who want to have the shelves well stocked, who are interested in consumers' needs and who are involved in the intricacies of retailing and marketing. Of course, any such balance will produce tensions within the collective, but, experience shows that, after working forty hours a week shoulder to shoulder, ideological differences become less divisive because there is a friendship and bond based on work.

Most collectives operate on consensus decision-making, meaning that even one person has veto power. Consensus decision-making is a good mechanism when decisions are very important (e.g., hiring another person), and when the groups are quite small. It helps to bring the participants together and everyone knows who has lent support to any decision by not opposing it. For decisions which are minor (e.g., number of brands of catsup to carry), majority decision-making might be all right because those opposed probably don't feel as strongly about the question and it permits meetings to be relatively brief. By the same token, however, one might say that minor decisions do not involve strong personal feelings and therefore are more amenable to consensus decision-making.

Another question is whether workers should rotate their jobs. This gets to the basic problem that even though a work structure may be non-hierarchical in theory, if there is a division of labor, there is usually a division of knowledge, and if one person has more knowledge of the enterprise than the others, then that person has concrete power over the other employees. The most obvious example is the bookkeeper. The person who keeps the books knows the reality of the enterprise. The rest cannot know it as well. Thus at meetings the group may decide to give $50 to a local political group and the bookkeeper might say that the bank account is overdrawn by $1,000 and they cannot afford to give $50 to anyone. It is important for everyone in the collective to at least know how to read the books so that they understand cash-flow procedures, so that they can understand how a business might be in debt at the moment yet in solid financial standing, why the initial loans for opening the business will put a burden on expansion for the first year or two, and so forth. It is probably important for each person to rotate through a number of jobs as an apprentice, to learn buying, wholesaling, bookkeeping, shelving and stocking, and publicity. After this knowledge is obtained, specialization can be useful. Some people like to do the buying, some like to work the cash register, some are good at writing newsletters. There is no reason not to have this kind of specialization, except if it leads to a monopoly of knowledge and information preventing the collective from making good decisions as a group about different aspects of the store's operation.

What type of business should one initiate? The most profitable parts of the economy are probably those that deal with liquor. By controlling liquor the state has made it very expensive. Therefore bars and liquor stores have a good rate of profit. If profit were the only consideration, this would obviously be the target commodity. But of course profit is *not* a consideration at all in making a self-reliant community. It is difficult to conceive of a liquor store being a good community gathering place or an educational vehicle for neighborhood reconstruction.

Other businesses come to mind. Laundromats might be good because they could combine a necessary chore with a spirit of community-mindedness. (Does every household need its own washing machine?) If it is big enough, a laundromat can be a meeting place as well, with a bulletin board, games, and good reading. Laundromats also have a high rate of profit, especially if there are good mechanics in the community who can keep the machines running. There is a high capital investment in machinery, but then the loan capital can be paid back quickly.

Food stores are a good business also. In many inner-city areas the large supermarkets are closing down because they no longer see food retailing as profitable there, because of high rents and, in poor neighborhoods, high insurance rates, and high theft rates. Such closings provide the opportunity for alternative stores. Food stores can be a good educational vehicle. Food is directly linked with health, consumerism, agribusiness, and chemicals. Finding that a community store has bulk items, that one has to scoop out raisins and nuts from large containers, that there is no packaging, permits people to remember that there is no need for individually sliced and wrapped food. Food stores have low profit margins, and make up for it with a high volume of sales. This means that in choosing a store one should be careful to choose a location that is large enough and has enough street traffic. People usually will not go far out of their way to a food store unless it sells specialty items. The fact that it is a community business can be helpful in attracting patrons, but probably will not cause people to leave other neighborhoods to shop there. In Washington, D.C., it has been discovered that a volume of around $15,000 per week (in the spring of 1974) was sufficient to repay start-up loans of $20,000, pay a work force of eleven persons about $100 for a forty-hour week, and still generate some money for other businesses in the form of low-interest loan capital. It is not easy getting to that point, and it can't be reached if the store space is so limited that shelves have to be continuously restocked, trips to wholesalers have to be made every day or two, and check-out counters are crowded and slow. People will not shop at a store which cannot keep its shelves stocked, or where they must wait an hour to check out.

A drugstore is also a good project for a community. Drugs are enormously expensive. And other non-food items have a much higher markup than foodstuffs. Therefore a non-profit drugstore can undercut by much more the comparable prices in other parts of town. Reductions of thirty to fifty percent below even discount stores is not uncommon in toiletries, contraceptives, and so on. Non-prescription drugs often have even greater possibilities for markdowns. Just by buying non-brand names and generic items prices can be slashed by as much as seventy-five percent. And, of course, if one can get a pharmacist to oversee the drugstore, then prescription drugs can be dispensed. In Kentucky, Maryland, and Washington, D.C., there is a substitution law, which permits a pharmacist to substitute equivalent generic drugs for brand-name prescriptions written by doctors. In no other parts of the country is this permitted, although bills have begun to come up in state legislatures, and we can be fairly certain that within a few years substitution laws will be widespread. What this means is that if a doctor has given you a prescription for tetracycline under brand name "X" which costs $3.50 for twenty-five tablets, you can get the pharmacist to give you brand "Y" which is the same thing although manufactured by a smaller company and selling for seventy-five cents for twenty-five tablets. The savings can be quite dramatic and can help to teach people the relationship of big business to personal health.

One problem with drugstores is their relatively low volume of sales. Perhaps, as is being done in Washington, D.C., a pharmacy should be run in conjunction with a food store, or a food store could begin to carry non-food items and then expand to prescription drugs. In this way the volume of the food store will carry the overhead, and the prices of non-food and drug items will attract a wide clientele to the store.

A hardware store is another possibility. This may not be as profitable a business as some others, since it also does not have a great sales volume. But in terms of education and community organization it has strong possibilities. A hardware store can have visual and three-dimensional displays showing people how basic machines work, how leaky faucets can be fixed, how to fix frayed cords, what a motor looks like. It can teach people to make their own household repairs while selling them the tools with which to do them. It is a way of meeting the technical people in the neighborhood. And it can easily expand into other areas, such as having service people who will fix machinery in the neighborhood while teaching people to repair their own machines at some future date. It can have a hotline service for advice on car repairs and machinery, and it can be a vehicle for teaching about new technologies, like windmills or solar collectors, that might spark the interest of some in the neighborhood. (Community technology, is explored in a later chapter.)

There are a number of ways to raise capital for such ventures. Conventional loans from financial institutions are one, but they are difficult to obtain because there is no credit and no financial stability among the participants. Also, loans made to small businesses often have such high interest rates that they put a very heavy burden on the development of the business in its early years. Individual loans can be obtained. Cooperatives raise money from membership fees and from selling shares. Collectives often sell coupons, which are later redeemable in merchandise. The denominations are usually $1, $5, and $10. It brings in a few thousand dollars if done properly, but is mainly useful to involve those members of the neighborhood who might not see themselves as being able to support the venture because they have no large amounts of available cash. The amount needed to open a business depends, of course, on the location, the nature of the business, and the vision. Grocery stores have opened and been successful with $40,000 in capital. Laundromats, depending on the number of machines and space available, need about $25,000 to operate in a financially secure condition. A hardware store might be able to start up with considerably less money because it doesn't need a large starting inventory.

Wholesaling, Trucking, and Processing

After the retail stores operate for a while, it becomes clear that in order to realize any large savings for the community, the businesses must raise their volume purchases and also take on as much as possible the associated operations of production, processing, distribution, and wholesaling. The food stores, for example, find that they can undercut large supermarkets in fresh produce and bulk items like nuts and raisins and tea. But packaged items like mayonnaise and catsup and cereals and tunafish are usually slightly higher in the alternative stores than in supermarkets because no individual store can buy in volume as Safeway or A&P can. In many parts of the country this situation has been partially resolved by retail community stores organizing together as a buying club to make purchases in large volumes. A natural extension of this — and again, what is being done in Washington, D.C. — is to develop a trucking distribution network, rent a warehouse with refrigeration facilities for storage, and make contacts with farmers in the area.

Volume ordering brings with it another aspect of the business operation. It leads to an outreach with other communities in a business arrangement that could lead to exchanges on other levels as well. This is discussed more fully in the chapter on inter-communalism, but a few words at this time might be helpful to complete the picture. In the Southwest there is a trucking cooperative that picks up fresh vegetables in Southern California, services the food warehouses in San Diego, and then goes over the mountains to Tucson, Arizona, to bring them produce. In June of 1974, talk began on a plan to link together the co-ops in Minneapolis, which have their own warehouses and a refrigerated semi truck, with the food co-ops in the Southwest. The truck would deliver grain to the Southwest and return with fresh vegetables to Minneapolis. The buying could be done in significant quantities to permit large discounts that could be passed on to consumers.

Another part of the business chain is the processing of merchandise. In some businesses, such as record stores, plant shops, or hardware stores, it might be difficult initially to think of producing the tools or plants or records locally (although it should be thought of somewhere along the line). Yet in food the processing stage costs relatively little and produces important dividends. In Washington, D.C., two people set up a peanut-butter processing plant in a local warehouse. The "plant" consists of nothing more than a couple of grinders. Their peanut butter undercuts organic peanut butter by a large margin and is competitive with the Skippy brand of creamy and chunky butters. Not only does this produce more income for the community by extending the number of people employed by the community itself, but it also brings another stage of production under the influence of the community. If the peanut butter is not good, the community might complain about the quality of the peanuts and might insist that peanuts of higher quality be used. This sort of complaint directed against Skippy or Sunkist would, of course, be meaningless.

In Minneapolis, Detroit, and Philadelphia there are grain mills which process wheat into flour. The protein content is much higher than usual, although there is the drawback that the flour must be used within a few days or it will spoil because of the oil content. Sometimes these operations are linked together, so that bakeries use the freshly ground flour, restaurants buy through the retail stores' buying federation, and so forth. In Tucson there is a juicer cooperative which can process high-quality juices (except for apples) more cheaply than the large companies can. Once again, because they contain no preservatives, juices must be sold quickly, but this is compensated for by having a much higher health quotient.

Food processing can be carried out at various stages of sophistication. The peanut-butter mill and the grain mill are primitive, fairly low-capital-outlay operations. Slightly higher on the scale is the "canning plant" sold by Ball Jars Corporation, a nonprofit branch of the Ball Company. The plant consists of two steam boilers, a juicer and pulper, racks and tables, everything needed to can almost anything. It fits in a room 25 by 25 feet and

costs $7,500. It will can up to 1,600 quarts per day at a cost of
about six to eight cents a quart. Food preparation and processing
plants, as they are called, have been in operation for a number of
years in third-world countries and on Indian reservations. They
were begun primarily to permit people in low-income areas to
take advantage of the low prices of fresh produce in season. The
price of much produce, for example, can rise five times between
June and January, but if the produce is canned in July it can be
"consumed" in January at the same approximate cost per quart,
plus a few cents. These plants can add to the "wealth" of the
community. They can be operated as a service to the residents, or
as an adjunct to the store's operations, or possibly as a community business themselves. Once again, these canneries can be
meeting places where people can exchange information about
canning and nutrition while using the machinery.

FOUR

Controlling the Local Economy:
The Neighborhood
as an Economic Unit

As the retail stores flourish and distribution systems develop, as processing plants open and repair shops begin to transform themselves into basic manufacturing facilities, an awareness of the neighborhood as an economic entity emerges. Concepts such as gross neighborhood product, or neighborhood balance of payments, become appropriate matters for research. Investigative studies begin to develop new methods to explore the underdeveloped-nation status of the community.

There are very few existing studies relating to neighborhood finance, and therefore those used in this chapter should be viewed as suggestive and preliminary, rather than definitive. However, the few that have been done support Milton Kotler's statement (noted earlier) that:

> The important features of a poor neighborhood are, first, the discrepancy between the aggregate expendable income of the neighborhood and the paltry level of its commerce, and, second, the discrepancy between the considerable tax revenue the neighborhood generates and the low level of benefits it receives in public services and welfare. In both cases, the neighborhood exports its in-

come . . . . Its present internal commerce is dependent, as is its level of public services, on commerce and personnel outside the neighborhood.

One of the earliest studies, done in 1969 by Earl Mellors, examined the Shaw-Cordozo neighborhood in Washington, D.C., a primarily low-income area with a population of 87,000. Mellors discovered that the area had an aggregate personal income of $144 million, of which $44 million flowed out in taxes and fees. And, according to Mellors' best estimates, only $34 million came back in services and public welfare, leaving an excess of $10 million going outside the community.

Many people have questioned both Mellors' methodology and his conclusions, but the figures themselves probably underestimate the toll taken on the neighborhood. Even the $34 million identified as money going back into the community goes mainly to people like police and teachers, who live outside the neighborhood and come in only to perform their services. Thus there is no multiplier effect from this salary output on the local economy. But more important, these stark figures do not and cannot take into account possible alternative expenditure patterns that might arise if the neighborhood controlled its own taxes. To give but one example: a neighborhood which controlled its finances might not pay out welfare in the same manner as the city or federal government does. Because those on welfare would also be friends and neighbors, the community might use the allocation to produce employment commensurate with the person's ability. The elderly who are good with children could be hired to operate a day-care center. Such a center could be partially supported by those who could afford to pay, and partially from this subsidy. The amount of savings this might theoretically give to members of the neighborhood depends on one's assumptions. Besides giving productive, pleasing work to a segment of our population usually cast aside and ignored, it would free up many mothers who could in turn become useful in other neighborhood ventures. The amount of money spent might well be exactly the same, but the returns would be very different. If 100 mothers, for instance, suddenly received free day care for their offspring and had the worry of their children lifted from their shoulders, the community might estimate it had gained about 200,000 hours of work a year. Or, to view it another way, presuming that the mothers were going to work anyway and pay for someone to take care of their children, the welfare payments to the elderly and unemployed could have saved these mothers, assuming three children each, about $30 a week or $150,000 a year in day-care expenditures. If we make a different assumption — that these mothers worked anyway and didn't pay some other person to take care of the kids — we must take into account the psychological damage if one of the older children becomes a substitute parent at such a young age, or the social problem of having kids grow up with no supervision — wandering the streets, hanging around with teenage unemployed or liquor-store companions.

To take another example, let's use the education budget. If a neighborhood controlled its school expenditures it might, as the New York City teachers' union has always feared, become parochial and racist and illogical. But it might just as well decide to orient local education to the needs of the neighborhood, to continue teaching the basic concepts necessary for public education, but to restructure the course content so it reflects local needs and diversity. High-school students interested in psychology could learn the theories of child psychology from a trained professional while gaining experiential input from the newly created day-care centers. Public-school science classes could try to produce products that reflect the needs of the community around them. In Walkden, England, for instance, a secondary school for girls has, under the direction of a progressive and creative schoolmistress, developed several inventions for the deaf and the infirm in their science classes. They are simple devices using basic scientific principles, and were invented by the twelve- to fourteen-year-olds because the mass consumer markets often overlook or ignore smaller groups of consumers such as invalids and the infirm.

While the science classes produce buzzers for traffic lights so that the blind need not be fearful when crossing the streets, urban planners could design sloping curbs for paraplegics, or redesign shopping carts so that they can be transformed into baby buggies or even scooters when not used for transporting merchandise.

The main point here is that, even if the money put back into the neighborhood approximates what is sent out in taxes and fees, we can still push toward neighborhood autonomy with a clear sense that it is not a self-defeating and Pollyannaish attempt to cut one's lifeline by "seceding" from the federal and municipal subsidy trough.

Taxation is only the first step toward a visualization of the neighborhood as a viable economy. A full-scale investigation of fiscal flows and what we might begin to call the neighborhood balance of payments must also be done. One such study, by Richard Schaffer, was done of the Bedford-Stuyvesant section of New York City, a poor area of 250,000 residents. Estimating capital flows into and out of the neighborhood, Mr. Schaffer concluded that in the case of Bedford-Stuyvesant there was a favorable balance of payments. The main reason for this was the huge input of public-assistance moneys from the local and federal governments. Schaffer's study tends to dispute Mellors' conclusions, but produces some interesting data in its own right. According to this study, the amount of money which flowed out of the community for drugs and gambling equaled the amount that came in as public-assistance payments. The government, by outlawing certain commodities the public obviously desired, created a monopoly distribution system and thus a great strain on existing community resources. The deficit caused by one arm of the government was made up by another arm pouring in public-assistance funds — and rigid rules and regulations, the foremost being, "Thou shalt not spend any part of this on drugs or gambling."

In low-income areas such as Bedford-Stuyvesant any survey of fiscal flows must take into account the pervasive influence of organized crime. A study done by Harold Lasswell in 1972 discovered that organized crime in Bedford-Stuyvesant, through its gambling and drug operations, was grossing more revenue than the federal government was collecting in taxes from the same area. Furthermore, the gambling operation in the area is the second largest single employer, next to the government itself. There are interesting parallels between the legitimate government and the illegitimate government in Bedford-Stuyvesant. They seem to work at times hand in hand. The legitimate government outlaws some activity, and organized crime moves into that sector of the economy. The legitimate government pours in welfare money which then goes into the illegitimate sector to engorge the coffers of organized crime. Part of those profits goes back into the legitimate governmental sector in the way of bribes, political contributions, and so forth.

Before we leave this side note on organized crime, we should note that it does do positive things for the residents. Sources in Bedford-Stuyvesant explain that many of the small stores in the area take bets and use the cash profit to extend credit to the large welfare population. It is the only way, they say, for the small stores to compete with the large chains. In addition the numbers runners and controllers are known to lend funds to their better customers who are temporarily short on funds (and the custom is that the loan is interest-free). Thus organized crime is apparently crucial to whatever credit economy exists in that area.

The development of retail and wholesale suppliers in the neighborhood and over the city has helped to control a part of the local economy. Funds that were previously going to people living outside the area, to hire outside people to work in the area, to buy merchandise produced outside the area, are now going to support a local economy wherever possible. This, however, is just the beginning. There are large amounts of capital that flow through and out of any neighborhood in the form of rents and increasingly high real-estate payments (which will be covered in the chapter on housing), taxation at both the city and federal levels, and savings in local financial institutions. In a typical low-income neighborhood maybe thirty percent of its gross personal income will go out in fees and taxes to different levels of government. The concept of taxation has changed tremendously since this country was founded. At one time a revolution was fought against taxation and there were many battles even after the revolutionary period against the state and federal tax collectors. Even up until the late 1800s, tax collectors were considered fair game for anyone, and the stories about tax collectors being tarred and feathered and ridden out of town on a rail were not all fiction. Taxes at that time, when locally accepted, were means to raise enough money to accomplish a social purpose beyond the means of any one individual, a way for people to pool money, time, and energy to create something necessary for the whole community. In contemporary America the tax has become a sort of tithe. We pay a percentage of our incomes for the privilege of living in this country with no expectation that we are going to receive any direct benefit from that payment.

On the neighborhood level, in order to begin controlling the fiscal flows within the community there need to be a number of different levels of education and institution building. First, there might be actual research studies which show how much aggregate income there is in any given neighborhood, how much is devoted to such things as gambling, crimes, fees, taxes, food, and so forth. This can educate the neighborhood into an awareness of its own resources and can also begin to give an overall picture of the "underdeveloped nation." Second, mechanisms could be developed to teach people how they can begin to redefine taxation and credit, and control at least to a minor extent the money they earn. This means the development of, for example, community sustaining funds, internal taxation mechanisms to service the neighborhood itself, and credit unions to capture a part of the savings in the area. The third step might be the establishment of a full-service bank, a neighborhood-development bank, which can fully involve itself with loans, savings, checking, and a number of other services for the community. Each of these steps has already been taken in different parts of the country, so there is some practical experience in the limitations and potential of each.

Community sustaining funds exist in Champaigne-Urbana, Madison (Wisconsin), Eugene (Oregon), Philadelphia, and Austin, to name just a few. They usually develop after the retail stores are established and after the idea of self-reliance has been carried to the stage of institution building. Basically, a sustaining fund is a tax on purchases at community businesses. The tax, usually ranging from one to four percent, goes into a general fund and the people of the neighborhood who have paid the tax vote as to where it should be spent. The tax is a regressive sales tax, but in most areas this is felt to be all right because it isn't compulsory: people can refuse to pay it if they so desire. It is also the only vehicle a neighborhood has for imposing such a tax. There is no criminal penalty attached to non-payment, no way to tax personal income, and no administrative mechanism for tax collection. In Madison, the sustaining fund has raised up to $50,000 in a year. In other areas the yield is more modest, ranging from $10,000 to $35,000 a year.

Although the basic principles of the sustaining fund are the same throughout these cities, there are differences which can become very important over the long run. The major questions are: How should money be collected? Who should be a member? Where should money go? In most cases the money is collected by an automatic "voluntary" tax; that is, the tax is collected unless the patron says no. This puts social pressure on the patron, but still leaves an out. In those funds where this principle is reversed, where the patron must first say yes, there is very limited yield per year. In some cases this tax is supplemented by fund-raising activities, by check-offs on wages where people are willing to do this, and by benefits. In a few cases the stores tax themselves, tax their gross sales volume rather than individual customers. If the stores are actually reducing their overhead revenue as a result, then it is a true retail tax. If they are merely passing on the tax by raising their prices one percent, it is a compulsory tax on all customers and should be treated as such.

Who should be a member? In some cases there is representation from various organizations in the city. In other cases those who pay the tax are members of the fund. In almost no cases is there open membership, where just anyone is permitted to vote on fund allocation.

Where should funds go? This is a crucial question, and has led to a number of internal conflicts. This is especially true in those cases where there are many ideological groups participating in the fund's operation, each with opposing politics. The optimum procedure is to have criteria clearly laid out as the fund is established, so that people know what kinds of projects they are giving their money to. Will money be given to service as well as business operations? Should the money only be loaned to businesses, but granted outright to service institutions? Does money have to go only to non-profit organizations, only to worker collectives, only to groups with certain politics? Can money go to political demonstrations or for legal aid or bail money? All these are questions that probably should be thrashed out before a fund is well established. Besides the obvious importance of defining the fund so that people know why they should give it money, it will also be helpful to make it distinct from the more common municipal funds, like United Givers, or Fund for Greater Detroit, which get most of their money from government-employee check-offs and give their money to a wide range of non-profit service organizations which come under the umbrella of social-service projects. Rather than trying to create a viable and productive new society, these funds simply replace the old charitable system, trying to help those who are needy without confronting any of the power and economic arrangements which might have caused them to be needy in the first place.

Any definition of a sustaining fund will of necessity change as members grapple with concrete decisions. Making things too specific at the beginning can only lead to trouble later on. But one rule that can eliminate later conflict is that the money may be used only for capital expenditures, not for overhead or salaries. This means that groups can request money to buy a mimeograph machine, a new freezer or electric saw, or a building, but cannot ask for salaries or telephone expenses. This rule tends to do two things. First, it makes people aware of the concept of community wealth — that wealth comes from productive facilities and that the more land, space, tools, and machinery the community owns and operates, the wealthier it is. Even if millions in foundation and government money are poured into the community, it cannot become viable unless that money produces ongoing and self-sufficient organizations. The poverty money in the middle sixties is a clear example of a literal flood of money which created jobs in low-income areas for a period of time, only to have the areas fall back into lethargy and disunity as soon as the subsidy was withdrawn. Second, the rule eliminates at least partially the internecine squabbles which have ruined at least one fund (Madison). Serious problems could develop if a choice must be made between supporting the salaries of a black organization as opposed to a white one, or a gay group as opposed to a women's group. But if the gay organization needs a mimeograph machine, if the hardware store needs a drill press, if the food store needs a bigger walk-in freezer, the community has the direct or indirect use of these tools. If there is enough money to purchase a building, several groups can reside there together. And after a year the tool or building is still available for the neighborhood to use.

Credit unions are another step toward controlling the wealth of the neighborhood and directing it toward community use. Credit unions, of course, are ubiquitous in American life. The first credit union was chartered in the United States in New Hampshire in 1908. Credit unions were chartered only under state laws until the Federal Credit Union Act was passed in 1934. In 1971, there were some 23,300 credit unions, with more than 24 million members and total resources of about $21 billion.

Credit unions are limited to groups of people having a common bond. Federal credit-union charters recognize three types of common bonds — occupational, associational, and residential. The first two are widely familiar; residential credit unions are relatively new. Occupational credit unions involve people who are employed by the same employer and work in that employer's related activities. Associational credit unions are for members of an organization who share common loyalties and mutual interests through that organization. Residential credit unions are for persons residing within a defined geographic area who have a community of interests, activities, and objectives.

Each of these credit-union groups needs a certain minimum potential membership to be granted a charter. For residential groups there has to be a minimum of 300 families potentially involved. This means that a neighborhood credit union, or a number of neighborhood credit unions, is a distinct possibility. In fact, such geographically based credit unions already exist, many having been established under the auspices of the OEO programs of the late 1960s. For chartering purposes an urban community should "be reasonably compact . . . . The population of the community should not greatly exceed 25,000."

A little-known aspect of credit unions is that deposits are insured in a manner similar to deposits in regular banks. This is true only since 1971 when Public Law 91-468 provided for insurance to a maximum of $20,000. (State-chartered credit unions can apply at their option and almost all of them have.) Therefore putting money in a credit union is just as safe as putting it in the Chase Manhattan Bank. Also, it will earn a higher interest rate than if kept in savings-and-loans associations. (Credit-union interest rates in mid-1974 were normally more than six percent as compared with five percent at local savings and loan associations.) Credit unions do not have checking accounts; they are similar to savings and loan associations, although somewhat more limited in what they can do with their money.

Credit unions can lend money to their members. It is a good mechanism for people to get mortgage money. Investors in the credit union are members. Although credit unions rarely operate like cooperatives, with each member having one vote independent of the amount invested, they still, because of their relatively small size, are open to membership participation and more amenable to their patrons' demands.

There is a definite process for organizing credit unions, with an overall authority either in the state or the federal government, depending on where one is seeking chartering. The process involves proving the economic advisability of the union, the fitness of the subscribers, the need for such an institution, and so on, and may take up to two years, but can take considerably less time.

The very exciting possibility is that credit unions may develop into full-service banks. This has only been done, to our knowledge, once in this country, and in that case it was a very old credit union which had managed to acquire a large amount of capital over the years and made the transition rather smoothly. In most other cases it will probably be difficult to accomplish. Credit unions can give neighborhoods valuable experience in dealing with financial matters, with bookkeeping and accounting. The difficulty is that most residential credit unions are quite small, with very little money on hand; therefore, they operate in small storefronts, or on side streets, not in ways conducive to bringing community support and building confidence.

The neighborhood-development bank is a new idea. No one to our knowledge has yet acquired a charter to start one. But there is a group which hopes to accomplish this goal, although it began by buying out an existing bank on the South Side of Chicago, called the South Shore National Bank. Chicago has unit banking, meaning there are no branch banks. The South Shore National Bank, located in a deteriorating section of Chicago, decided that it could not afford to stay there any longer; deposits were declining and the neighborhood was declining. The bank made application to move downtown. The neighborhood, through the complaints of powerful community associations, protested bitterly at the proposed closing of its only bank. The city review board refused to permit the closing, and a group of community-minded investors moved in, bought the bank, and began making plans for a neighborhood-development bank.

Ronald Grzywinski, the leading figure in this sequence and currently president of the bank, had previously been vice-chairman of another bank in Chicago, and so had the experience, the ability and the standing in the financial community to raise the money needed and reduce the amount of cash required. The previous owners of South Shore were able to get permission from the Illinois State Comptroller to reduce the bank's capital by half to $3 million, and the number of shares outstanding from 200,000 to 100,000. This lowered the amount of money Mr. Grzywinski had to raise to purchase the bank. In addition, American National agreed to provide interim financing to him of up to $3.2 million to acquire the shares.

The South Shore Bank will be only one part of a holding company called the Illinois Neighborhood Development Corporation, which has filed an application with the Federal Reserve Board to get permission to form a holding company and acquire South Shore. The holding company would own two non-bank subsidiaries. One would be a for-profit corporation to back investment projects in South Shore; the other a not-for-profit development arm to channel government and private grants to community groups and projects. Ironically, such a community-minded bank was made possible by recent changes in the Federal Reserve Board guidelines which were intended to tighten controls on bank holding companies that have strayed far afield from regular banking activities. In outlining the limits of permissible activities, the Board mentioned that holding companies "possess a unique combination of skills and resources to deal with a number of the nation's ills," among them being community deterioration. This was the crack that the South Shore Bank has barged through.

In talking with Ron Grzywinski, one gains an idea of how useful a bank can be for the neighborhood. In this case, when the bank was bought out, it was in the red. One year after the change in management, through hard driving policies, it is in the black. The neighborhood has about 80,000 residents, and is deteriorating according to all reports although there is still a strong middle-class section. The South Shore Bank is the only bank in the area. Its assets are about $43.5 million. Mr. Grzywinski thinks that a one-percent profit on gross assets can be reasonably expected from a bank after the initial period of operation. This would mean that the South Shore Bank, after another year or two, should be able to generate almost half a million dollars over and above all costs but dividends to shareholders. If the investors are willing to forego those dividends, that money can be put back into the neighborhood for housing rehabilitation, construction, and community facilities.

A bank or holding company as adventurous as the one planned in Chicago is, of course, an enormous undertaking. But at this state in the neighborhood's development there should be an awareness of identity, a developing consciousness that there are enormous resources even in the poorest neighborhood which, if directed toward internal improvements, could have a significant impact, and a network of institutions and community organizations which are beginning to make an impact on municipal-government structures. The South Shore National Bank is an example of a group buying out a specific bank. That permitted them to sidestep the cumbersome process of asking for independent chartering. Similar situations might occur in many neighborhoods, particularly if they are deteriorating.

But in many other cases a group interested in starting such a bank or holding company will have to go through the complicated process of getting a charter. They can ask for a charter for a national bank or a state bank. There are two major steps involved. First, one gets a certificate which gives permission to raise capital for the bank and outlines what conditions need to be met in order to receive a charter. Step two is getting the charter after having met the conditions. The conditions are numerous, but the most important one is that a given amount of deposit capital must be raised in a specific period of time. In order to get permission to raise capital a group must prove that there is a reason to have another bank, that it can serve a necessary function, and that it has a viable chance of succeeding. Chartering boards are interested primarily in the economic viability of the enterprise. If they think that the neighborhood cannot support a bank easily they might deny permission, or might increase the amount of start-up capital necessary. One can figure on about one million dollars of commitments necessary for such an enterprise, although this figure can be lowered if the neighborhood joins in the petition and a good case is made that the neighborhood can further develop from the creation of a unique institution such as a community-development bank. The entire process could take a year and a half, and there are few shortcuts. Obviously, attracting that sort of investment capital means going to churches, foundations, and certain corporations, stimulating them with the idea of capital being used directly in a community for improvement. This will not be easy, because, as noted above with respect to credit unions, money has its own dynamic. Many people will not understand why, if a bank is a viable institution in the neighborhood, there isn't already a bank there. If the bank is going to give high-risk loans, why won't it go bankrupt? Doesn't money go where it can make a significant return, and why can a bank change this merely by willing it so? These are important questions, and go to the very heart of banking and finance, and must be confronted straight-on in discussing the investment with prospective financiers.

Although bank chartering boards look at the economics of banking as their primary criteria, they are impressed by community support. This has perhaps been more important in the case of Chicago's bank, when community protests stopped the board from granting the bank leave to close its operations in South Shore, but it can also be significant in getting a charter granted to a nascent operation. If the group petitioning for a charter has previously operated a credit union, it can demonstrate its competence in financial areas and, depending on the assets of the credit union, might have a great bargaining lever to attract new capital.

FIVE

Neighborhood Housing

For most people their home is the single most important aspect of their lives. For those who buy a house it will be the largest single purchase in their lifetime. For those who rent, the money going out will be even more, the equivalent of a tithe of twenty-five percent of their salary every month for the rest of their lives.

On the other hand, real estate is big business, perhaps the biggest single industry in the United States. With the skyrocketing cost of land, the shortage of adequate housing, and the closing of other tax loopholes while leaving real-estate write-offs a tax accountant's dream, real estate remains a bonanza for investors, real-estate operatives, and developers. In every city, real-estate interests, which are inevitably tied into local banking business, and even religious circles, are a powerful constituency.

So, when we talk of land and housing, we talk of the very lifeblood of many cities. Without ownership of the house you live in or the turf you walk on, without some sense of security that you will not be evicted without reason, that the rent will not rise beyond your means to pay it, that the building won't be torn down to give way to some nonresidential use, no real community can exist.

As a neighborhood begins to re-establish a sense of community, of mutual aid, and of local productive enterprise, it will naturally improve its atmosphere, attracting people to the area who previously would not have come. It is a sad but all-too-common tale. Real-estate speculators do not make their money in those areas of a city which are already highly valued, nor in those sections which are destitute, down-trodden and crime-ridden. They concentrate their interest and activities on the twilight zones, those sections of the neighborhood which they call "in transition." This means those areas which are beginning to become attractive, where middle-class or white interests are beginning to move in and land values are beginning to rise. Since real-estate people have their ears close to the ground, they can come in early and sell quickly, capitalizing on the land boom. In and out. Buy a house for $15,000 and sell it in a month for $25,000.

Land speculation not only hits individual landowners, but apartment dwellers as well. When an area becomes more attractive, renters get terminations of their leases and are turned out of their apartments to make way for higher-priced clientele after the apartment has had a "face lift," or to make way for heavier construction and the change to condominiums. Land speculation, of course, runs its course, peaking quickly and then leveling off or even turning downward. But in the meantime it has destroyed any possible "value" neighborhood real-estate has had. Once upon a time, so they say, there was a value to a house. That value was based on the neighborhood in which it was located, true, but it was also based on the beauty of the house, how structurally sound it was, what needed to be done in the way of remodeling, and, perhaps most important, what the seller thought was a reasonable price. After speculation has occurred, it is extraordinarily difficult to return to those days. In Washington, D.C., an elderly woman whose husband had died decided that her three-story townhouse, in which she had lived for forty years, was too large to care for. She decided to move to an apartment and rent the house. She spoke to a friend about it, saying that she thought $400 was a reasonable monthly rent. That was what it would take to cover her apartment costs and depreciation on the house because of other people living there. A week later the *Washington Post* newspaper ran a two-part series on land speculation in her area. Her friends told her that the house was worth a lot more than $400 a month. A month later she rented it to a group of seven people for $800. The moral is that there isn't any reasonable rent once a neighborhood becomes marketable.

But there is another point, which was made earlier but which bears repeating. The twilight areas of any city are the places where those who might be interested in neighborhood reconstruction go to live. This is the area where community based on ideology meets neighborhood based on geography. It is the edge of the ghetto. Rents are fairly low. And groups living together can get landlords to rent to them. Since rents are low, people can live communally and support themselves with part-time jobs or get involved in the neighborhood, creating counter-institutions or service organizations. Unfortunately, such groups have recently been the vanguard in the real-estate land speculation game. Groups can pay more rent than a couple can. They drive rents up all over the area, bring in their friends, change the nature of the community. This, in turn, makes the neighborhood more attractive to other, albeit richer, members of their race and class, who follow them, buying up buildings, reconverting town-houses into apartments. And, little by little, the nature of the neighborhood changes.

It should be added here that another significant factor in a neighborhood's control over its own land is the availability of mortgage money. It is common practice among city banks to "red line" neighborhoods. A red-lined neighborhood is one which has been considered a high-risk district. Mortgage money does not go into those neighborhoods. In fact, in city after city, study after study, the same situation occurs: local savings go to buy houses in the suburbs where the houses have better collateral and the houses are newer, smaller, and in better condition. The same process occurs in these twilight areas of the city. Low-income people cannot buy their own houses in the city because banks will not lend them money. The first whites or middle-class people to move into the area also find it fairly hard to get mortgage money, although not as hard because they have good jobs and the houses are, after all, going at a low price. As mortgage money becomes available, that is, as the appraisers sent out by the banks begin to realize that the neighborhood is no longer "in transition" but has, indeed, become a viable entity, it still goes to the then flood of new entrants because they are better risks than those who already live in the neighborhood. The traditional residents cannot win. First they are a bad risk because their neighborhood is run down. Then they are too poor to compete with their richer cousins when the neighborhood gets built up.

Land speculation is not the major evil, perhaps, but it certainly is the most dramatic, and should be clearly understood. For if the neighborhood tries to deal with the problem of rising land values after it has already made efforts to develop community, it cannot win. Only if it begins to have the community buy its land first, or in the beginning, can it hope to have any measure of success. For at that time land values are low, and there are no fortunes to be made in quick speculation.

As has been said, land speculation is the most dramatic, although not the major, force toward rising land values. Apartment houses, for example, have their own internal financing dynamic pushing for higher rents. Peter Barnes, economist and author, has described a typical case in *The New Republic* in April 1974:

> Suppose a landlord buys a building for $100,000 with $20,000 down and an $80,000 loan. After several years the building is worth $120,000 and the principal outstanding on the loan has been reduced to $60,000 thanks to the tenants' monthly rent checks. The landlord then refinances the building by taking out a new mortgage, say, for $100,000. He pays off the $60,000 still left on the old loan and pockets the $40,000, in effect cashing in the equity his tenants built up for him, plus part of the gain from the building's rise in value.
>
> Wondrously, he pays no capital gains tax on the $40,000 because it is in the form of a loan rather than the proceeds from sale. And because he still owns the building, he continues to receive his month-to-month profits and retains title to future appreciations in value. The only problem is that he must make higher payments on his new, larger loan, but again this is easily solved by raising rents.

What prompts a landlord to refinance his building? Not only the profits gained from the new loan. Barnes goes on to explain the practice of allowing large deductions for depreciation of buildings, even though their value in fact appreciates over time:

Consider what happens after landlord A buys a large apartment house and enjoys its hefty depreciation and interest deductions for several years (like depreciation deductions, interest deductions are concentrated in the early years of ownership because loan repayments contain more interest than principal at first). When landlord A's tax deductions drop too low, he sells the building for a capital gain to landlord B, who begins his own top-heavy sequence of depreciation and interest deductions. Landlord A in turn uses his profits to buy another building on which he can get those juicy front-end deductions once again, and both landlords raise rents to cover the higher financing costs of their new loans.

According to Barnes, about half the annual investment in real estate goes into buying or refinancing existing buildings, rather than into putting up new ones.

So the cards are stacked against the neighborhood. Financial considerations push for higher rents, land speculators move in as the neighborhood becomes more attractive, and zoning boards rarely take into consideration the needs of the community. What, then, are the tools that the neighborhood has at its disposal for stabilizing community life and giving people the security that comes from knowing that they will be able to afford to live in the area for years to come?

One tool is the zoning board. Zoning is a bureaucratic jungle which swallows up the unwary. Zoning boards are never elected. In some cities there are boards of zoning adjustment, and planning bodies, and still other bodies, all of which participate in deciding whether the neighborhood is to retain its viability or not. The rules and regulations are bewildering. There are zoning changes and variances (which are temporary zoning changes);

there are sub-categories in each zoning area which are confusing yet important for each citizen to understand, such as special zoning, which is often used as a foothold to get a later change in zoning densities.

Zoning began in the nineteenth century as a means for keeping out nuisances in a community. The first cases had to do with the desirability of having laundries or brick ovens in residential areas. In New York City in 1916 the first comprehensive zoning code was established. It went beyond a regulation of land to a regulation of buildings and population. It regulated the height and density of structures and it regulated population. Since then the zoning process has become even more cumbersome and unwieldy, and has often been the central battleground for neighborhood residents.

Common sense dictates that zoning should be done at the local level. All courts and legislative bodies have recognized that fact but, unfortunately, have defined "local" to mean municipal. Thus, cities of several hundred square miles, with millions of residents, will have one zoning board and one planning agency. Zoning should be done by elected officials on the neighborhood level. Neighborhoods are almost by definition places which people have identified as communities. They have geographic boundaries and borders.

Zoning hearings should be held in the neighborhood that is going to be affected. Zoning is above all a political decision. It is true that experts are needed to give testimony about the effect the proposed changes will have on traffic congestion, on employment, on light and air in the neighborhood. But it is the people who live there who need to take that advice and decide how they want to design their neighborhood. Making zoning changes political will, of course, mean that changes come about much more slowly. Yet there is no evidence that the rush to change has produced a better way of life in America, and much evidence that it has led to the deterioration of our communities. Besides, zoning law teaches us that, at least in principle, if not in practice, the person asking for the change is supposed to bear the burden of proving his case; that is, the law assumes that stability is an important enough consideration that it must be outweighed by the needs of new structures or uses of land and buildings in the area. Unfortunately that wise dictum is rarely followed in zoning cases, where the local real-estate and business and banking interests have the lawyers, the engineering staff, the contacts, and the perseverance to get their way.

Neighborhoods should, and can, push to have zoning devolved to the neighborhoods. Already there are advisory neighborhood councils set up in various parts of the country (to be discussed more fully in the chapter on neighborhood government), which have a formal link to the city in terms of local planning and zoning. They do not actually make decisions, but have a formal input into the decision-making process and their opinion carries a great deal of weight.

Even without having control over zoning, a neighborhood can still mobilize itself to stop the encroachment of high-rises, gas stations, parking lots, and office buildings. It can do so in at least three ways. One is to mobilize community residents to make known their complaints about the proposed change to members of the local political establishment and to the businesses or individuals involved in the dispute. Second, they can argue their case before the zoning board, using their numbers and petitions of the community to make clear that at least the residents in the area feel that the proposed change is not beneficial to the welfare and public interest of that community. Three, they can go to court to appeal any decision of the zoning board.

In recent years, because of the mushrooming complaints of citizens' groups, the courts have given citizens several important tools with which to fight zoning changes. The most important one is the environmental-impact statement. If a high-rise is going to be built under federal funding, it needs to demonstrate that it will not affect the environment of the neighborhood adversely. Therefore, environmental-impact statements or traffic reports prepared for the opposition are important documents to get hold of beforehand and utilize in preparing a rebuttal.

The difficulty with zoning cases is that often the builders will move in and have a *fait accompli* even with neighborhood opposition. This has been true in the case of parking lots in Washington, D.C., and probably in other parts of the country.

The builder submits an application for demolition of several buildings he has acquired. The permit is granted, the tenants are evicted, and the buildings are demolished. The residents only know of what is going on as the tenants begin to exit or the bulldozers come in. By then it is too late. While the zoning board might have refused a zoning adjustment for a parking lot in a residential neighborhood where there were buildings and residents living in them, it rarely refuses such an application when there is only a dusty piece of ground. A neighborhood would be well advised in this respect to establish a committee to keep informed about permits for demolition as well as about zoning variances that are coming up. It is very important to have knowledge beforehand in these cases. Otherwise the builder is always one step ahead. "Judge," he argues, "I've spent one hundred thousand dollars tearing down those buildings. I've got a building permit, hired engineers, and started construction. And now you're going to tell me I can't go ahead and build on that piece of land? It's not fair. Why didn't you warn me beforehand?" And, of course, it is a very persuasive argument.

Zoning boards, however, can sometimes be helpful to citizens' groups. In Washington, D.C., in the spring of 1974, the citizens of one neighborhood were able to get approval by the zoning board for down-zoning most of the neighborhood. This meant that the parts of the neighborhood which were zoned for buildings up to ninety feet high were suddenly restricted to building heights of sixty feet. It was a tremendous victory, and even more so because the zoning board made its decision on the basis of the need to provide "for stability and the preservation of the area's special character and ambience." It was one of the first times that a decision was made to down-zone a neighborhood because current zoning would lead to the destruction of that neighborhood as a viable place to live. Such sweeping decisions can give neighborhoods breathing space with which to develop a comprehensive plan themselves. Without such a decision the growth of special zoning areas, multi-family buildings, office buildings, and then high-rises gradually overcomes the best of efforts by residents.

There are other tools the neighborhood can use to maintain

its character and stability. Most of these need to be used in conjunction with the city, but such a move will often have the support of other neighborhoods experiencing similar problems. One such tool, and one used more and more frequently in recent years, is that of rent-control ordinances. If rents can be stabilized, then it is difficult for the landowners to move through the refinancing procedure or move a different class of people into the area's structures. Rent control, however, is a difficult area itself. If not handled properly, it can set up still another bureaucratic agency, unresponsive to citizens' needs, controlled by the city's real-estate interests, and yet with the sanction of legislative approval. If not written properly, rent-control laws can lead to deteriorating buildings. Landlords, rather than raise the rents, will allow the services in the building to decline, and get their profit that way. In the long run this will lead to a decline in the property value of the area. The best rent-control law, in our judgment, has these various aspects: First, it puts the base period for rent control a year or two before the bill becomes law. That prevents landlords from raising their rent quickly before the bill becomes law. Second, it sets up an agency, once again on a neighborhood level, which can be helpful to citizens who want to complain about a landlord but are afraid of retaliation. This is especially important because if the base period is two years before the bill becomes a law, the landlords themselves must provide the information about rents, and tenants might be very wary of disputing those figures later on. Third, there is a penalty for the deterioration of services. This might mean that if there is a determination that the building has been run down, there is a lowering of rents in that building. And, finally, there should be strict mechanisms for permitting landlords to raise rents because of remodeling or rehabilitation of the structure. In Washington, D.C., the proposed rent bill, not yet law, states that rehabilitation is defined as structural repairs which have raised the value of the building by fifty-one percent. This prevents the common practice of sanding the floors and putting up new wallpaper, and then raising rents substantially.

Direct action is also possible by tenants. Tenants' unions are common in many cities around the country, and they have

developed a substantial body of law and practice in their years in
action. In most cities housing codes are rarely enforced, and when
they are it is with a pat of the hand. In even the most strict cities a
landlord who has thousands of violations might have to pay a fine
of only $2,000 after years in court. Therefore violations have had
little impact on tenant-landlord disputes. The law has consistently
upheld the right of the landlord to do almost anything he wants
with his building. Landlord-tenant courts are mockeries of justice.
The question is, "Did you pay the rent?" If not, you are guilty.
Harassment, housing-code violations, or the like, are not considered reasons for withholding rent. In most cases it is difficult, if
not impossible, to go to court to get a landlord to fix up a
building.

But times are changing a little bit. The shortage of housing,
the fact that the middle class is beginning to feel the pinch, and
the skyrocketing costs of rentals, have prodded the courts and
legislative bodies, as well as tenants themselves, to move in
different directions. One of the primary tools that has been used
by tenants is the rent strike. This means that tenants withhold
their rent from a landlord who has not made repairs on a
building. The rent often goes into an escrow account, which
means it cannot be touched by the tenants and that it will go to
the landlord, but only when the sought-after repairs are made. In
some instances, these sums of money become very important
bargaining tools. In Berkeley, the tenants in two buildings owned
by the same landlord went on a rent strike for many months and
won the right to bargain collectively with management. The next
year, when the contract was up the management refused to
renegotiate with that union, and another rent strike was held. The
strike went on for nine months, with the landlord taking the
tenants to court. In the interim there had been a decision in the
California Supreme Court which stated that rent could be
withheld if the structure was not "habitable," and it defined
habitable as being substantially in compliance with applicable
housing-code regulations. It was an important decision for it gave
tenants a tool to force landlords to make repairs on decrepit
buildings.

In addition, tenants are beginning to demand jury trials all across the country in tenant-landlord cases. Juries, made up primarily of other tenants, are wary of deciding against people whose situation they know quite intimately. In the nine-month rent strike in Berkeley, the jury decided on a technicality to throw the landlord's case out of court. The judge was astonished, making the comment in court that the tenants would have to pay their back rent "sometime." Two of the jurors came to the victory celebration held afterward by the tenants' union. In Washington, D.C., black tenants are now asking for juries, which would be composed primarily of blacks in their same situation. Landlords became so frightened that they immediately drew up new rental-contract forms which state at the end that the tenants have promised not to ask for a jury trial if any disputes arise. Such a contractual agreement, it turns out, is not legally binding, but indicates the potential that jury trials have in housing cases.

In some instances, admittedly rare, the amount that has been placed in escrow has turned out to be so large that the tenants have finally bought out the landlord. That is, the combination of the huge escrow and the withholding of the rent forced the landlord into bankruptcy and was followed up by an offer from the tenants to form a cooperative and purchase the building.

Tenant unions suffer from lack of contact with other tenants in the vicinity who face the same problems. Tenant unions now are trying to get people in many apartment houses or individual dwellings, especially those owned by the same corporation or individual, to pool resources and join together. In many ways the tenant unions are following in the steps of the labor unions of the 1930s, spreading out, organizing different branches of the same factory, bargaining collectively with management.

There are other possibilities which have been offered by knowledgeable people in the housing field. They need legislative approval for implementation, but are interesting in their potential. One is a transfer tax on buildings. This has already been implemented in Vermont in rural areas. It means that if a person holds land or a building for a short period of time he is taxed greatly on it; the longer it is held, the lower the transfer tax. This might not curb speculation in rural areas because land there is often held for many years, even by speculators. But it might thwart land speculation in urban areas, where land speculators try to get in and out as quickly as possible.

An intriguing proposal has been presented by Ed Kirshner and Eve Bach of the Community Ownership Organizing Project in Oakland, California. That proposal combines cooperative ownership of apartment houses with local subsidies from a city to produce a well-thought-out and integrated housing program for cities. It is based on the cooperative. All included units would be financed under a single mortgage. The mortgage would be held by a non-profit cooperative association, which would in turn be owned by resident members in the form of shares — one share per residential unit, one vote per member. The cost of a share would be nominal, maybe equivalent to a monthly payment, and if a member moves, the co-op would buy back the share which would be resold to a new resident member at no gain to the co-op. Members would make monthly payments to the non-profit cooperative corporation equivalent to their portion of the total mortgage payment plus expenses.

There seem to be many advantages to this plan. Cooperative members are considered owners under the law, and therefore gain the advantages American tax law gives to home owners. They can deduct that portion of their monthly payment which represents property-tax payments and interest on the mortgage. Also, in some states, the cooperative members are assured a property-tax deduction as owner-occupants. Kirshner and Bach estimate that in California this step alone would reduce housing payments by $15 to $25 a month.

Add to this the fact that cooperative members would be owners, protected from rising housing-market prices and free of arbitrary landlords. They would be protected from rising housing prices because the perpetual mortgage in the hands of the corporation would never be refinanced. Members would have all the advantages of ownership except one — they would not individually acquire direct equity in their housing mortgage.

At this point in their proposal, without subsidies, Kirshner and Bach estimate that the necessary household income for one of their houses would be lowered from $14,300 to $7,400. Yet they go on to suggest that the city become involved in subsidizing the program through a number of methods at its disposal. Cities can get involved in financing the cooperatives through use of their pension funds, or carry-over reserve funds. They can utilize their ability to borrow money by issuing tax-exempt bonds, thereby lowering the interest rate and the subsequent mortgage. And, finally, they can use an index loan, a commonly used device in Sweden but unknown here, which ties the loan to the cost of living and has as its primary advantage the fact that finance costs are low initially and change only at the same rate as the cost of living or other price indices.

With all of these subsidies, plus cooperative maintenance of the dwellings, and the low vacancy rate for cooperatives, the cost of the housing would drop even further. It is a plan which combines control over housing by those who live in it with municipal underwriting of financing and elimination of vulnerability to rising market prices of housing. Even in the beginning, such a program would lower prices substantially. Over the years, moreover, the rents would go down as the mortgage was paid off and the comparable rents in unprotected housing would skyrocket, causing the prices of the units to drop even more substantially.

We have gone through a number of different tools that are available to neighborhood residents to fight the scourge of land speculation, skyrocketing land costs due to financial considerations, and the kind of redevelopment that destroys communities. It might be good to end with a brief discussion of one of the finest, yet most controversial, tools for taking land and housing out of the capital market. This is the simple procedure of preventing any one person or corporation from owning more than two or three dwellings, of which one must be owner-occupied. This is, perhaps, the most controversial housing issue in the United States. Even non-rich people resent it, for theirs is always the dream of owning many houses, a summer home in Majorca, a winter apartment in the city, a farm in rural America, and a string of rental properties on the coast. A dream is a dream. One cannot deny that dream with statistics. It is true, however, that although a substantial number of Americans are in the process of paying off a mortgage on a house, a very small number have two houses, and only an infinitesimal number have more than that. It is absentee ownership which causes most of the problems in housing because it is absentee ownership which separates responsibility from profits. The complaints of individuals about rats or no heat, about homes being turned into condominiums, and the complaints of neighborhoods about encroaching office buildings, all usually hinge on the fact that an absentee owner is using land and housing as a profit-making mechanism, and the needs of the neighborhood, or even of the individual buyers or renters, are peripheral to that goal of making higher profits.

It is probably impossible to begin writing into law provisions prohibiting ownership of buildings which one doesn't use, but it is high time that a debate was begun in this country on such a policy, because without it the tools described above will be mere cap pistols in the war against profits from housing that is being waged across this country.

SIX

Neighborhood Government

It is clear today that the great experiment of our cities is a failure. We must return to a scale of government which is comprehensible to our citizens. By developing neighborhood government not by fiat, but by an organic evolution from community organization, we can develop a sense of community through the state and a sense of individualism and neighborhood through the nation. To date the centralization of government has destroyed community self-management and citizen participation. We must reverse this trend and develop our cities along the lines of neighborhood government and interneighborhood cooperation.

— SENATOR MARK HATFIELD

Local liberty is the cornerstone of democracy. Its importance was historically paramount in post-revolutionary America. Alexis de Tocqueville, the famous French observer of America, declared after traveling through the country in the early 1800s, "I heard citizens attribute the power and prosperity of their country to a multitude of reasons, but they all placed the advantage of local institutions in the foremost rank." Thomas Jefferson, even while President, supported a political system in which most power remained with local wards or neighborhoods which were, in effect, miniature republics on their own.

Yet over the past two hundred years, we have seen the erosion of local liberty and the extension of centralized authority.

Thirty cents of every dollar we now earn goes to support governmental programs and bureaucrats. One out of every six workers in America works for some level of government. There are more public bureaucrats in this country at this time than there are production workers.

Although the franchise has been extended to almost every adult, the power of an individual vote has diminished considerably. In 1800, there was one representative for every 30,000 people, about the size of a contemporary big-city neighborhood. Currently there is, on the average, one representative for each 300,000 people. In the last federal election only fifty percent of the potential electorate even registered to vote, and fewer than half of them voted. In other words, less than twenty-five percent of the potential voters cast ballots. Even when participation rises, no one seems to be involved in the voting process. Elections are rarely fought on issues anymore. Elections, like television, are designed to be bland. The trick is not to make anyone mad. A story about Hubert Humphrey, the perennial candidate who most people agree is a thoroughbred campaigner, sums it up. On a television program he was asked about the then current Nixon administration. He called it the worst since William McKinley, and then quickly added, "Of course, I have nothing against William McKinley," just in case there were some survivors of the Spanish-American War in the viewing audience.

In only a handful of states is there the possibility for citizens to generate initiatives or referenda on their own, developing local issues and then voting on them. There are even fewer states which permit recall elections of officials who have broken their campaign promises. No one really expects anyone to keep their campaign promises. We vote on style, and the vote is an expression of confidence and faith that the candidate will be a good president, or governor, or mayor when he or she assumes office.

Yet elected officials represent only the tiniest tip of the governmental iceberg. They are far outnumbered by the millions of appointed and civil-service officials who are not responsible to anyone, and whose tenure in office seems permanent. Bureaucracies which are established to deal with temporary situations live on far after their reason for existing has disappeared. Finding the "responsible" official has become a national pastime, whether it is the person to whom you should complain about rats in a house or the federal official to whom you can talk about the food-stamp program.

Neighborhood government, on the other hand, can be based on an assembly of citizens within the community who directly participate in decisions. Neighborhood government, common sense tells us, is closer to the people and therefore less susceptible to the abuses of power which isolation brings.

But we have learned to fear the judgment of our neighbors. As much as people complain about big government, there is a belief that, by being so remote from our homes, national government will not interfere very much in our *private* lives. People admit that the abuse of power might be greater on the federal level, but the personal impact, they hope, will be less. It recalls the argument about white-collar versus blue-collar crime. The white-collar criminal steals more and hurts the society more, but does not physically threaten individuals as much as the blue-collar criminal who climbs into the bedroom window in the middle of the night. In the same way, national government breeds inefficiency, corruption, and excesses, but local government, it is said, breeds fear. This difference, of course, is more in the mind than in reality, since the federal and state and municipal governments *do* interfere in our private lives. Regulation is the rule of the day, and the private rights of those who might be against the status quo are never respected by any form of government.

The fear of one's neighbors has grown along with a dependence on central authority. At each national crisis, whether it is depression, internal riots, or external war, the federal government grows stronger, presumably to deal with each crisis. After a while, people began to depend on the government to get things done. One can criticize the government's programs, but never the government itself. Government replaces "the country" as the focus of patriotism.

As wealth grows, as a transient lifestyle increases, and as our jobs take us out of our communities, we begin to lose touch with our neighbors. We don't know who they are, or what they think, or how they live. On the other hand the mass media tell us more than we want to know about our representatives, our politicians, even our federal bureaucrats. There is a familiarity in the names of those who lead the country and a sense of confidence in their ability to surmount crises. From time to time there is talk of the need for "new ideas," or "new blood," or even "new leadership." But rarely are there many voices that ask for less leadership and more citizen participation on the local level.

The Vietnam War was probably a watershed in this period of government sanctification. Those who supported the war never seemed to have a good argument. It was always, "The government has access to information that we don't" or "You don't think the government would get us involved in something this serious without good reason?" The opponents of the war said that the Vietnamese were not our enemies, that they never attacked us, and that we saw no reason to kill them. It was a case of common sense versus faith in government leaders. Even Watergate has seemed more a question of how to recapture that feeling of confidence and faith in the government that the Vietnam War caused so many to lose, rather than a deeper questioning of the entire structure of government in this country.

There are currently many leaders, and followers, who know that something is wrong. The federal government has tried to give back some money to states and cities through revenue-sharing procedures. Mayors have set up little city halls and some cities now have advisory neighborhood councils plugged directly into the formal city apparatus. These, however, are not, as citizens constantly rediscover, actual delegations of power to local levels. Rather, they are means for extending the apparatus of the city or the state or the federal government, so that people can feel that their complaint or requests are being channeled to the right official. As State Representative Hugh Carey of New York, running for Governor in a Democratic primary stated classically: "I'm a great believer in decentralization. But that doesn't negate the Governor's responsibility to set policy at the top and to audit the spending at local levels." The structure of government is not touched. Rather, it is to be made more efficient. But there is an alternative.

From ancient Greece to modern New England there is a strong tradition of democracy based on direct participation by the people in the area. In Greece, cities had provision for 30,000 citizens in their assemblies. Although rarely did that number show up, the point is that many people can effectively participate in decision making. There was a Council of Five Hundred, which was the chief executive body, and which prepared the agenda for the assembly and oversaw financial and foreign affairs. This council was chosen annually *by lot* from a roster of citizens over thirty years of age.

Consider for a moment this description of Greek democracy more than 2000 years ago:

> Nearly all legal cases were tried in popular courts, for which there was a panel of 6000 citizens chosen annually by lot. . . . Popular juries sometimes as large as five hundred, uninstructed by judges, heard the plaintiff and defendant present their own cases, then gave their verdict by majority vote. . . . That same method of selection (by lot) applied to the lesser administrative offices, including the Commissioner of Public Works, the Police Commissioner and the Anchons, who had charge of formal state occasions and presided over the law courts. . . . Officials serving on various minor administrative commissions were closely watched by the people and were subject to frequent investigation. Every month a committee of the Council audited their accounts and certified whether they should be retained in office; their record was reviewed at the end of their terms, and charges brought against them by any citizen were given prompt and thorough attention. . . . There were no appointive offices and only in the case of the Board of Generals did the people actually elect their representatives rather than choose them by lot, the principle being that military and naval strategy was a highly technical job which

could not wisely be entrusted to any person whose lot might
be drawn.*

If that description of society doesn't appeal to you, if you
think such participation must have been ineffective, or too
burdensome, or some such other thing, then we doubt that the
whole idea of neighborhood government will appeal to you. It will
be your lot in life to continually give to a centralized government
almost total authority over your purse, your home and your life,
and then try to create mechanisms which can protect you from
abuses of power by that very same entity. At best you will succeed
in maintaining institutions which cost billions of dollars to
maintain and do absolutely no productive work except the work
of ruling *your* life.

There is a crucial point there about government. Government, no matter how enlightened, is not productive. It does not
grow food, does not produce electricity, does not build houses or
pave roads. It does order the printing of money, but only our own
sweat and toil make that money worth anything. The authors of
this book live in the District of Columbia, where 40,000 of 800,000
residents work for the District government, and many more than
that work for the federal government. When David Morris asked
his college political science class if they could foresee the time
when *everyone* worked for the government, they unanimously said
yes. In some mystical fashion, it was felt, the government could
provide for all. (It is, we might add in passing, that same mystical,
almost religious, faith that permits us to march boldly into a
future where an increasing number of people will be retiring on
private or government pensions or social security and a decreas-
ing number of people will be generating societal wealth. Common
sense once again can tell us that this is an impossible situation.
But once again we will hear that there are classified memos which
clear up the whole problem, that there are hundreds of Ph.D.
economists working on the government payrolls who *must* have
taken that into account. After all, it can't be that our government
is stupid.)

* Walter R. Agard, *What Democracy Meant to the Greeks* (Gloucester, Massachusetts: Peter Smith, 1960).

Since the government is not productive, but in a literal sense merely pushes paper around, or distributes checks, or makes up rules and regulations, or checks up on people, it can function only insofar as we agree to give our real wealth for its upkeep. The power to tax is the power to keep the government afloat. What we need to do in this country is to decide how much government we actually need, and then, how much we are willing to pay for it. In the next chapter we will see that this inventory of needs is necessary in the material sector as well. We must get back to taking stock in our own situation, deciding how much we need to maintain a desirable existence.

Neighborhood governments can evolve in many ways. They can grow out of existing community organizations. Saul Alinsky gained his fame in Chicago in the 1940s setting up People's Organizations. These included representatives from many existing community institutions, including street gangs, churches, labor unions, and civic associations. Another way is to develop a government directly from an assembly of individuals, rather than representatives of existing organizations. This has been done in Washington, D.C., in the Adams Morgan Organization. Finally, a neighborhood government can be imposed in a fashion from outside the community. This final method may be good or bad, depending on how it is done. As mentioned above, there are now neighborhood advisory boards in several cities around the country. In many of these, there is a financial subsidy given to underwrite the expense of the board, and this creates a community council even where none existed before. Senator Hatfield has written a bill, now in committee, which would permit people to give up to seventy-five percent of their income tax to the neighborhood government. People in his office see this as potentially giving up to seventy billion dollars directly to our communities. The bill sets forth procedures by which one can define a neighborhood, including asking the people, looking at the demographic breakdowns, and seeking out natural boundaries like a river or a freeway.

However the neighborhood-government idea arises, there will probably come a time when it decides to define itself as a government. For example, coalitions of groups may combine to fight land speculation, or to testify on pending legislation before the city administration. If these organizations are effective, they will begin to realize, as we have already suggested in the chapter on land and housing, that one needs to constantly monitor neighborhood land transfer and other developments or else be consistently behind the eight ball in the struggle. As the stability of the organization increases, other committees might form, looking into neighborhood recreation, neighborhood crime, or city-neighborhood relations. At some time, people will begin to ask how to formalize what is already happening, and how to give the informal committees some political clout with the city or other organizations. This is the point when serious discussion of the procedures for government takes place.

The most vital question, of course, is whether the form of local government will be representative or participatory. A representative form would simply extend the methods of the past into the future, having some sort of elections for the leaders of the newly formed coalition committees. If the decision is to move in such a direction, then the notion of neighborhood may be stricken from the agenda. What is being formed is simply a traditional government in which the leaders may well be local folk but whose roles will be little different from those of any other bureaucrats. The regular politics of privilege and position, of wheeling and dealing, are inextricable in such a form. The neighborhood is no more near to liberty than ever. Only the leaders have been changed. And the leaders, no matter how friendly and familiar, are not the neighborhood. The neighborhood is the sum of its people, not the elite of its leadership.

Assembly government, participatory democracy, town-meeting democracy, are some of the names of the real alternatives and the real base for local liberty as opposed to local leadership.

Will the people of the neighborhood participate fully in the decisions that affect their lives — no matter how time consuming, no matter how troublesome? Will they be full-time citizens or just now-and-then voters?

When the people, or at least many people, in a neighborhood finally decide that they want to participate in politics and not just delegate power to politicians, then community politics begins, local liberty becomes a possibility, and the debates over neighborhood government sensibly begin.

In the initial discussions there are several questions that are of major importance. One concerns the role of the assembly (the people of the neighborhood). Will the assembly have all rights, or only some of them? Will members be representatives of community groups or can individuals be represented? If individuals can be members, do they need to have lived in the neighborhood for a certain period of time? How often will the assembly meet? Should it have officers?

The second major question is, should there be an executive council, and, if the answer is yes, how should it be chosen? Should there be some group which oversees day-by-day developments in the community, digests information for presentation before the assembly, and does the dirty work necessary to maintain a presence in the community outside of assembly meetings? If so, should these council members be chosen by lot? Should they be elected by the entire assembly? Should they be elected by wards within the neighborhood in elections held directly in those wards? Should the council officers be heads of the various committees? Should they be paid?

If the decision is to have an executive council, the next questions concern the ability of the assembly to maintain control over the council people. If they are chosen by lot, how long are their terms? If elected, can they be recalled? If so, in what procedure?

Finally, and of course, of most importance, what kinds of powers should the neighborhood government have? This question is somewhat moot because, at least until a bill like Hatfield's passes, these "governments" will have almost no governmental power. None of the existing advisory neighborhood councils are given the right to tax. None has political power. None has direct legislative power. So the choices are very limited. Still, this delineation of powers is important because it begins to spell out what kind of government people in the neighborhood want. It might be good to paint a picture of the ideal form of government, assuming the neighborhood had complete power — and then of the practical form of government under current circumstances.

As Saul Alinsky once noted, democracy means that we believe that if we give people real power, they will most of the time come up with the right decision. Democracy is, after all, a great risk, and one of the greatest risks of all is that people will freely vote to give it up. But in local liberty that is up to the neighborhood itself. And the enduring advantage of a decision made in a neighborhood is that it affects, basically, just the people who made the decision.

A government made up of representatives from various organizations has advantages in that it can claim to speak for many more people than normally come to assembly meetings. Also, since those various organizations will themselves be doing constructive and active work in the community, their deeds and accomplishments can reflect favorably on the competence and stature of the fledgling government. The disadvantage is that this and all other representative systems separate the people from the government. On a neighborhood scale there may not be a need for representatives. Also, existing organizations tend to have their own hierarchy, and if the representatives are chosen by the existing leaders, the rank and file may have little voice in, and therefore little respect for, neighborhood government.

In almost every case, however, from that of ancient Athens to present-day town meetings, the assembly has decided to have an ongoing group administer everyday affairs. It is useful to have some group which can prepare position papers, contact experts in various fields, and set up the assembly meetings to run smoothly. But giving up power over administrative matters to an executive council means also giving up power to this council in real concerns. It is a natural extension. The council, if elected, might begin to feel that it *represents* the community much more directly than the full assembly does. If the assembly meets very rarely, such as once or twice a year, with an agenda established by the council, it will be difficult to discuss matters fully and vote on them competently, so increasing power rests in the council. In one experiment with neighborhood government the council, which was elected, quickly became embroiled in bickering over who had said what on behalf of the entire organization. The argument for an elected council was that the organization would have much more prestige if it held local elections and had officers with a rank. But as soon as the council was established, the committees became inactive. By taking on symbolic power the council had undercut the real productive power of the organization. Those committees still active began to incorporate and split off from the organization, deciding that the need to clear everything with an obstinate council had restricted their flexibility. Yet they felt anguished because by moving from the organization's umbrella they were losing the political clout that they had had vis-à-vis the city or landlords or other external agencies.

If an executive council is established, it is generally a good idea to limit its term to six months, or one year, and to have general-assembly meetings fairly often. Even monthly assembly meetings should be useful since any neighborhood generates enough new gossip and hard news in a month to fill the agenda of several hours of meetings. The continuity which meeting every month can give and the sense of cohesion and solidarity which just talking things over produces are extremely important. This is even more true in those neighborhoods where there are many different cultures, age groups, and races living close together. In these neighborhoods the assembly government plays the crucial role of having people understand each other's problems and opinions.

Recall and initiative provisions are not new in our state constitutions, although not many states honor them. The purpose is to get out of office by formal procedure a recalcitrant official, and to permit citizens to bring up issues themselves. It is a good idea, for example, to have a provision in the bylaws which permits items to be added to the monthly agenda if ten members of the organization sign a petition, and that another item can be added to the agenda at the last minute, that is, during the meeting, if two-thirds of the people vote yes. This allows time for printing up agendas before the meetings, and also stops the meetings from being overly long on account of a crowded agenda. But it permits flexibility when an important issue comes up at the last minute, one that most in the community would want to discuss.

Since our neighborhood governments, at least in the beginning, will have no formal powers, they will be as powerful as the respect they hold in their neighborhoods. They can propose clean-up campaigns, can ask people to shift their money from banks which do not invest in the area to ones which do, can testify on behalf of the community at city hearings, can establish informal citizen patrols in high-crime areas, and can hold bazaars and picnics and do research into local issues. The primary purpose of the government is to begin to bring neighbors together under a unified umbrella organization, to synthesize many of the disparate activities going on in a neighborhood, and provide a forum in which to debate major decisions about the future of the area. The power of the neighborhood is the power of active residents. And that is the way it should be.

Democracy, however, does not begin and end on the governmental level, even in neighborhoods. Political life can, and should, be extended into many other areas: participation of residents in the adjudication process, in neighborhood courts; participation in planning decisions in local zoning commissions; participation in production decisions in worker collectives. All these are extensions of the basic desire to permit people to control their own environments.

We have already discussed the nature of worker collectives. The workplace is where one has the least power, yet where one spends the most time. One's place of work is a central concern of life. And the workplace is the central productive unit of any society. Having free elections in the society, yet no democracy in the workplace, is having an illusion of power. Anthony Wedge-wood Benn, Secretary of Industry under the Labor Government in Britain, said it well in a pamphlet written in 1970:

> The claim is for the same relationship between govern-ment and governed in factories, offices, and ships as was finally yielded when the universal adult franchise brought about full political democracy, or what it might be more helpful to rename "voters' control". . . .
> On the face of it the perils of yielding "production by consent" when we have already survived the far riskier experiment of "government by consent" would seem less daunting. It would have been, on the face of it, more logical

if the experiment in democracy had begun with industry; and only then, when proved successful, extended to government.

Certainly there is no more reason why industrial power at plant or office level should be exclusively linked to ownership of shares, than that political power should have been exclusively linked to the ownership of land and other property as it was in Britain until the "voters' control" movement won its battle.

This democracy can be extended whether the organization is a factory or a white-collar institution, whether it be a local government office or a non-profit institution. Worker democracy means that secretaries, janitors, middle-level managers, and paraprofessional personnel all have an equal say in how the work environment is structured. It does not mean that all workers have the same intelligence, or the same skills, or the same experience, just as democratic political elections, where one person has one vote, don't assume that everyone has the same understanding of issues, the same experience, the same level of intelligence. It does mean, however, that these decisions affect each person in more or less an equal way, that each person has the ability to participate knowledgeably in decisions affecting his or her environment, and that to do things any other way is to lead to a frozen class structure and an aristocracy.

Because the neighborhood assembly works through voter control, it can educate the neighborhood people about worker control. It can support organizations that change their internal structure to permit employees more say and influence, and can establish new enterprises on the principle of equality. Neighborhood people can point to more than the common-sense proposition that if one has a say in how the work environment is structured, a better workplace will result, which will lead to a better state of mind and a better product. The neighborhood assembly can point also to studies demonstrating that worker control leads to higher productivity. Many of these studies come from Chile, Yugoslavia, and China, but they are appropriate to Western capitalist countries as well. Seymour Melman, Professor of Industrial Engineering at Columbia University, studied twelve enterprises in Israel, six of which operated on an egalitarian basis in kibbutzim, six of which operated on a traditional hierarchical structure outside the kibbutzim. Those that operated cooperatively, Professor Melman discovered, had 26-percent higher productivity of labor, 24-percent higher productivity of capital, 115-percent larger net profit per production worker, and 13-percent lower administrative costs.

This last figure, the reduction of administrative costs, demands one further comment. The figure would probably be higher in the United States today; in American industry the number of administrators per one hundred productive workers has risen from ten in 1899 to thirty-eight in 1963. Making the workers bosses means needing fewer non-working bosses.

Government makes law. But bureaucrats, judges, and policemen mete out the punishment, decide who should be arrested, and often mold the written law in their own idiosyncratic ways. Democracy is not complete without giving people some control over the judicial system. Jury trials, which are under attack currently in this country, are one way to do this. Another way would be to try to bring law and justice down to the neighborhood level, where people can explore its function, change its mechanisms where necessary, and change existing legislation to meet prevailing local conditions. But neighborhood courts definitely do not seem an idea whose time has come. The fear of one's neighbor's judgments is too strong. Although in this country one's neighbors tend to be the most highly educated people in the history of the world, we are afraid that neighborhood courts will become kangaroo courts, open to petty jealousies and personal rivalries.

Ironically, however, by avoiding the judgment of our neighbors we invite and get the judgment of rich, remote politicians and planners whose morals we have seen exposed, whose mistakes we suffer widely, and who treat us all, increasingly, as mere numbers in a computer printout.

Although we may not see neighborhood courts in the near future, we are, however, already hearing murmurings about them. People have established their own vigilante patrols in apartment complexes in New York City because the police are not on the streets. Citizens in many cities are upset because the criminals seem never to end up in jail, committing dozens of crimes while out on probation. Liberals are concerned that the jails are becoming training schools for crime, and that preventive detention in our city jails and federal prisons is rather an education for a lifetime of crime. Police commissioners and even state officials are talking about halfway houses, in the communities themselves, where prisoners would be sent to be rehabilitated in a community atmosphere. Everyone agrees that under our judicial codes the punishment almost never fits the crime. Plea bargaining is a common fact of life in our overloaded courts, and the average black person can count on getting a far greater sentence than his white companion, even for the same crime.

Even the definition of crime is changing. A study done a couple of years ago discovered that almost ninety percent of the people surveyed admitted to having, at least once in their lives, committed a crime for which they could have gone to jail.

Sometimes the neighborhood "crimes" don't fit in anyone's book. The constant hassling of women as they walk down the neighborhood's streets is difficult to stop by calling a cop, because that is not listed in the criminal code, or at least is not one of those ordinances often enforced. In one Brooklyn community, neighbors effectively stopped kids from riding their scooters down the street by barricading the street. In Washington, D.C., one night a friend came by madder than hell. He had been selling a person a pound of marijuana and that person had pulled a gun, taken the pound, and about fifty dollars. What could he do? Certainly not call the police. The decision was made to post the picture of the thief on all neighboring streets (since he was known), telling people what he had done (obliquely of course) and asking that no one associate with him. Furthermore, it was decided to invite him to a community party where he would be confronted and made to give back the money and the loot. In the intervening week before the confrontation was set, he broke into another home, stole money, not marijuana, and was arrested.

At a more broadly significant level, middle-class and working-class neighborhoods have begun to experiment with the return of the most basic police power — the protection of life and limb — to the neighborhood itself. The experiments are no ill-tempered excursions into mere vengeance and vigilantism. They are painfully decided moves of survival against street crimes against which regular police have proven ineffective. Citizen patrols of high-crime neighborhoods are underway. Escort services for people having to walk home late at night are available in some neighborhoods. In neighborhoods in both New York City and Chicago, there is an agreement that everyone carry a whistle and blow it whenever trouble develops, with the neighbors being pledged to respond by calling the regular police, blowing their own whistles, taking whatever steps they can to prevent a crime.

A neighborhood court could be a place of first resort, with limited judicial powers, which could adjudicate simple disputes, like family quarrels, or small-claims disputes, or hassling on the street. It could also be the source of creative punishments. In a neighborhood court in Cuba, a waitress accused a customer of yelling at her. The court could have punished the man with labor in the community garden. But, after some discussion, they decided that he did what he did because he did not understand the difficult nature of the waitress's job. He was sentenced to work one week as a waiter in the same restaurant.

A neighborhood court could also teach citizens what real and humane law is all about. Most citizens come in contact with the law in traffic court, and with the traffic citation. In traffic court, you are judged guilty unless proven innocent, as any person who has tried to argue a case knows; legal niceties are not the rule of the day. A neighborhood court could help to demystify the legal process, which has become so obscure to the average citizen. In Detroit, Justin Ravitz, Judge on the Recorders Court, holds sessions on Saturdays when citizens are invited to his court to hold mock trials, to learn how to view a trial, what the law is all about, and how it provides important insights into individual rights and due process. In Judge Ravitz's court, the audience stands only for the jurors, the people, not for him. A lot of the mystical aura disappears, and what is left is good, direct justice.

Unless Senator Hatfield's bill passes, any neighborhood government will not have access to large amounts of money. Even if it were given the power to tax, its constituency might overrule that power. The power to tax can mean the power to spend in arbitrary ways. Even under close public scrutiny a budget can become an undecipherable maze when it grows too large. As we mentioned in the chapter describing sustaining funds, taxation at one time was a voluntary giving of money in order to fulfill a larger social purpose. It has now become a sort of tithe, which one pays each year for the privilege of living in the United States, and there seems little rhyme or reason to it anymore.

Funds can be raised directly through contributions. This is a time-consuming process, but it can provide real contact with residents and provide the basis for an ongoing dialogue about the activity of the neighborhood government. In Chicago the Citizen's Action Program (CAP), has used door-to-door solicitation very effectively, raising tens of thousands of dollars each year in this manner. Going door to door permits them to couple fund raising with informal education, telling the people what CAP and its affiliate agencies have done, how that has helped the city and the neighborhood, what a person can do to help, by giving time or energy to its efforts. It is not a good idea to equate the amount of money earned with the amount of support the "government" has, because bad times, inflation, and other events can restrict the amount of extra money available. However, even in our poorest neighborhoods there is "extra" money floating around and, as we have seen in an earlier chapter, in these areas organized crime, through its numbers games, often is the major commercial enterprise. If the people choose to support organized crime, taking their one-in-a-million chance of winning the pot, over supporting effective neighborhood organizations, which presumably are offering them better odds at improving their living situation, it is time to knock on more doors and do more educating.

It is in the debates about neighborhood government and the extension of democracy into all areas of life that the neighborhood will undergo its most decisive phase, exploring questions of self-reliance and local control in a way not previously done. The debates will be bitter and forceful, for the citizens are in fact discussing the foundation blocks for a new society, a new form of government arising parallel to the old forms. All the latent fears about the ability of people to control their own lives, the need for outside experts, the need for bigness, for those monthly social-security checks from nameless bureaucrats, will rise to the surface. We have become so used to dependency that even the idea of local government gives many the chills.

But even if people should choose to make decisions about local resources by themselves, they will need to confront an even larger question. For, as we noted above, a government does not create wealth, it merely channels it, taps it, directs it. A neighborhood cannot become self-governing in a concrete sense unless it produces wealth itself. Otherwise it becomes parasitical, living off someone else's wealth, or else becomes beholden to external institutions for contributions to its cause. Not until it can use the respect and energy that its members are willing to give it to meet many of the basic needs of the community can it begin to be a true democracy.

Neighborhoods cannot survive by themselves, nor would they desire to do so even if they could. But it is just as clear that our communities can be a great deal more self-reliant than they have been. It has been the theme of this book that community control and local liberty can only be retained if they stem from a productive base. There must be partial economic independence or else the democracy becomes only an illusion. The clearest example of this is the company town. While the people have the right to vote, everyone recognizes that a vote against the employer risks the loss of one's livelihood, one's house, and one's standing in the local community. Just as the American government depends on the productive wealth of the nation, so the neighborhood government depends on the productive wealth of the community. How far can our neighborhoods travel on the road to self-sufficiency? It is to this question we now turn our attention.

SEVEN

Neighborhood Production: The Limits of Self-sufficiency

> Beginning with the new technologies of the Industrial Revolution, the veneration of size has come to take on the character of a mystique, and, like most mystiques, it has come to enjoy an independent life of its own. The danger is that the size mystique will continue to grip men's minds long after the circumstances that originally gave rise to it have disappeared.
>
> — Dr. John Blair
> former Chief Economist for the Senate
> Subcommittee on Anti-trust and Monopoly

Independence, whether of neighborhoods, cities, or nations, requires a material base. Communities can realistically attain a measure of autonomy only when they can begin to physically sustain it. Can a neighborhood of 30–45,000 people, or less, generate its own energy, grow its own food, manufacture its basic necessities? What are the limits of self-sufficiency for communities in which we live?

Economies of Scale: Manufacturing

The veneration of bigness penetrates every part of American society. Nowhere is it stronger than in the area of manufacturing

115

and production. The one hundred largest corporations (of some quarter-million which exist) control over sixty percent of the total corporate assets in this country. In industry after industry there are either publicly sanctioned monopolies, as in broadcast and telephone communications, or oligopolies, as in petroleum, automobiles, breakfast cereals. Conglomerates, combining unrelated business activities under one corporate roof, have been growing rapidly since 1960.

Conventional wisdom holds that larger firms are a natural, even a welcome, extension of business activities, and that they should be encouraged. Such concentrations are said to bring with them efficiencies that lower consumer prices. The reality is that prices grow as concentrations grow. The truth is that bigness brings with it higher profits. Also, it is apparently true that bigness breeds slothfulness, that creativity and ingenuity are submerged, in the largest firms, to the goal of profitability, that with their influence in distribution and advertising, large corporations can create markets for their most convenient and profitable items rather than bothering to make products that people genuinely need. Their most imaginative efforts are in marketing, not in production of high-quality goods. Even the large profits of huge corporations may not be a sign of business acumen and efficiency. Many large enterprises get their profits as a result of their political influence, through tax write-offs and subsidies, import quotas, and defense contracts, not through competition in the marketplace.

One of the best studies on economies of scale in production is by Barry Stein, a business consultant and economist. He notes that even the largest corporations, with assets of hundreds of millions of dollars, operate from relatively small production units. In 1963, for example, the average production unit in single-interest firms was only 91.4 employees, rising but slightly to 93.8 for conglomerates. Moreover, these figures included all employees, and not merely production workers, so they substantially overstated the actual situation. (In 1963, for example, when total manufacturing employment was given as almost 17 million those classified as actual production workers were only 12 million.) Stein concludes: "There is thus a strong case to be made that efficient manufacturing industry need not be large. Indeed, if those powerful and successful organizations saw benefits to be gained by larger facilities, they would presumably build them."

There are many studies which indicate that the larger the production of a corporation, the lower the unit cost (up to a point) and therefore the lower the price per unit produced. But these studies have not found that the price increases which would result from smaller operations are very large. That means that if 10,000 units are produced instead of 20,000 units, it doesn't follow that each unit will cost twice as much. One of the reasons for this is that production costs are only a small fraction of total costs. According to Stein, the costs directly associated with the physical production of a product constitute less than one-half and often as little as one-fifth of the final costs. Thus, even if there are certain disadvantages to smaller-scale production, we must take into account the fact that these will be translated into relatively minor final price increases. For example, if a firm produced 100,000 cars per year instead of 500,000 per year it could raise production costs by 15 percent. But, with production costs only one-third of the total costs, the price to the consumer would have to rise only 5 percent. Mass production, in short, may no longer have the dramatic effect on prices that we have for so long supposed it would have.

The trend in modern society has been to separate the production of basic necessities from the places where those products are consumed. We have paid dearly for this separation, and at no time are we paying more dearly than today. As early as the late 1920s Ralph Borsodi, in his book *The Distribution Age*, sounded the warning. He noted that the centers of food production, for example, were moving farther away from the population centers. The basic cost of an item was no longer substantially represented by the amount spent in producing it. More and more significant was the cost of delivering it to the consumer. A typical breakfast cereal, for instance, cost 21 cents of each total cost-dollar to grow and another dime for processing. The other 69 cents went into marketing, retail profit and distribution. Today the same percentage holds true in the food sector. We spend twice as much getting the food to our table as we do in growing it. This situation is sure to get worse for, when we look at the production of food in terms of energy, the imbalance is even more severe. It takes five to ten times as much energy getting our food to our tables as it does to grow it, and with current energy prices rising we are beginning to feel the burden of having moved food production out of our communities, only to have to process it and truck it back in.

The advantages of economies of scale in most industries are dubious. Even where they are claimed to be substantial, they must be weighed against the disadvantage of having lost control over the production process itself. Stories about corporate indifference to human welfare abound. Even in the publicly regulated sectors this indifference is appalling. One recent horrifying example is the story of the elderly couple in upstate New York who had their heat turned off because they hadn't paid a bill. They died from the cold.

But the lack of influence over corporate decisions goes much further than this indifference and callousness. In many communities and small towns there is only one major employer, and that company makes decisions on whether to leave or stay, based on national and multinational profit criteria, not the needs or welfare of the town itself. A neighborhood or town which is dependent on a corporation cannot be more than superficially involved in controlling its own wealth, or making decisions about its future. It can tax that corporation, but not too much, or it will move away. It can ask it to stop polluting the rivers so residents can use them for recreational purposes, but it cannot demand this or else the corporate headquarters might decide that that site has become too expensive for future operations. It can ask the company to stay in town rather than pull up stakes and move, but only if it can offer something in return, and that often means reducing the very taxes that provide the town's services.

It is almost common knowledge by now that large corporations do not produce a superior product. General Motors in recent years has recalled about as many of its cars for defects as it has produced, and shows no signs of introducing better quality as a production technique. In a dramatic demonstration of the declining quality of our food supply Congressman James Burke of Massachusetts confronted Secretary of Agriculture Butz in 1974 over Butz's opposition to a proposal to give a tax credit and free seed to those who might want to plant their own gardens. At one point in their argument Burke took a tomato recently purchased at a local store and dropped it on the table top . . . and it *bounced*.

Finally, whenever we speak of economies of scale, we must include a discussion of the most basic question of all — what do we need? Not what do we fantasize about, or what will we buy, but what do we need? Corporations rarely address themselves to that question. It is not what they are all about. They are interested, on the contrary, in creating new needs to establish new markets and make higher profits. Drug- and grocery-store outlets, for example, carry some 6000 new products a year, more than twice the figure of ten years ago, and it is expected that during the 1970s a further 120,000 products will be introduced in supermarkets alone. As Stein puts it, ". . . 55% of all items sold there in 1970 did not exist in 1960, and 42% of all items then available have disappeared." Now think. What products now on your supermarket shelves have you found so much more worthwhile than the products of ten years ago? Which products are vital? Which are merely venal and frivolous?

Unfortunately, when politicians have tried to redesign our economy, they have started with the basic premise that in any redesigning we need to maintain the rate of growth and the sheer physical output of this society. During a meeting a group of avowed Marxists who had been working with automobile workers in Detroit, trying to organize them in opposition to their union and company, were questioned about their ultimate goals. They responded, "To take over General Motors." "What then?" they were asked. That was enough, they answered; the workers would control production and share in the wealth they themselves have produced. That was said to be "the revolution."

Yet, if we see General Motors as a part of the problem, and the multiplication of steel-bodied, internal-combustion-engine vehicles as contributing to our societal breakdown, a mere change in ownership would not necessarily mean real social change. Such change involves other questions. What kind of transportation system do we want? What kind of food production is needed for good health? How much energy does it take to fuel a satisfactory standard of living? And what, beyond mere numbers, *is* a good standard of living?

New Technology and Decentralization

Grappling with these questions means exploring the alternatives now available. This means examining new technologies that have come to prominence since World War II. For, in fact, many of our institutions were built when technological innovations, distorted by war, produced larger concentrations of economic power. Now they are like over-armored dinosaurs, standing in the way of more local and flexible technologies. When steel, for instance, replaced wood as a major structural material in the last century, it required a much greater capital investment in factories, not for simply technological reasons, but also for reasons of profit efficiency as envisioned by capitalist planners. Plastics, reinforced concrete, and other materials, which are rapidly replacing steel, require less technological capital and have so far avoided the concentrations of ownership which have characterized steel. Even *within* the steel industry innovations are pointing to decentralization. No less an authority than *Fortune* magazine noted recently:

> Those famous old economies of scale which demanded gigantic equipment and blocked the entry of small would-be competitors are greatly diminishing in importance. Small companies, emboldened by steel's "new economies" are streaming into the industry, setting up regional, even local plants, splintering the business into smaller pieces — and making money.

John Blair, quoted at the beginning of this chapter, describes this same process happening in almost all areas of the economy. The new technological advances are neither labor intensive nor capital intensive, he says; "they are knowledge intensive." As he writes in his brilliant textbook, *Economic Concentration*:

> With plastics, fiberglass and high performance composites providing high strength and easily processed materials

suitable for an infinite variety of applications; with energy provided by such simple and efficient devices as high-energy batteries, fuel cells, turbine engines, and rotary piston engines; with computers providing a means of instantaneously retrieving, sorting, and aggregating vast bodies of information; and with other new electronic devices harnessing the flow of electrons for other uses, there appears to be aborning a second industrial revolution which, among its other features, contains within itself the seeds of destruction for concentrated industrial structures.

What does all this mean for neighborhood development and the future of cities? It could mean, quite simply, that we may now be able to choose which way we want to go, whether we want to rely on outside forces and their dense concentrations of power and capital, or strike out for ourselves locally.

The most dramatic example of this choice will probably occur in the area of direct conversion of sunlight into electricity. It is commonly written that we are at least fifty years away from the time when photovoltaic cells will become competitive with fossil-fuel-powered generators as efficient sources of electricity. Recent events, however, belie this pessimism. A small corporation in Maryland, for example, has managed to lower the cost ratio of photovoltaic cells versus fossil-fuel electrical generation from 100:1 to 7:1. The president of this corporation thinks that the figure can be lowered to 5:1 within a couple of years, and that it should be competitive with fossil-fuel-generated electricity by the end of the 1980s. These projections assume that the cost of fossil fuels will remain relatively steady during the next ten years, a very conservative assumption. The advances achieved by this corporation have required investment capital of around $750,000 and a labor force which has been recruited virtually right off the streets. The firm not only does research and development, but markets its solar cells, testing them in the field.

There is the probability, then, that solar cells, which can be made in small neighborhood facilities and which will last almost indefinitely and can be placed on roofs to supply a major part of residential electrical needs, will become available within the next fifteen years. Right now, however, the largest corporations and the federal government are subsidizing and pushing for the introduction of nuclear-energy plants all over the country. These plants will be located outside cities, will generate enormous amounts of radioactive wastes and thermal pollution, and will be far removed from any effective public local control.

Both systems will take at least fifteen years to establish. This is a typical lead time for urban planning. Given the cost and adverse effects of setting up nuclear-energy technology, neighborhoods interested in future planning could reasonably demand that their tax money be spent in subsidizing solar-cell research and development to be done right within the communities. This could be done in a contractual agreement with some company, with the neighborhood being able to ride piggyback on new technological breakthroughs in return for its subsidies, and then being able to manufacture its own solar cells with the experience and expertise gained through the R-and-D period. This is not at all fanciful. As mentioned, one corporation produced its breakthroughs with less than a million dollars in venture capital, and it is making a profit.

In Washington, D.C., a subway system is planned. At the height of its operation, according to its planners, it will carry only 15 percent of the commuter traffic coming into the city. It will be completed in the mid 1980s and will cost anywhere from $4–8 billion. This figures out to between $1500–3500 for every man, woman, and child in the metropolitan area. If such an expenditure is brought down to the neighborhood level, $45–100 million would be available for transportation research and development in a community of 31,000. This is a fantastic sum, and only for *one* neighborhood. It could be multiplied with one neighborhood working with solar collectors, and another with windmills, another with plastics production, another with computers, another with in-house toilet systems, another with electric-vehicle production. The point here is that the money is available; it is the ingenuity to diversify its use that is missing.

The new technologies are knowledge intensive. They need personnel trained in the new sciences who are competent to keep up with new advances in the field. They need people with special knowledge about new equipment that is coming on the market. This kind of expertise, of course, is not found in every neighborhood. This, however, doesn't mean it could not be nurtured. Our urban educational systems are massive, with thousands of trained scientists at work in them, millions of dollars worth of equipment, and hundreds of thousands of trained, or semi-trained technicians in the classrooms. There is no reason why some of these educational personnel and resources could not be diverted into useful community technology applications. Also, although we noted that the new technologies are knowledge intensive, we also noted that they are not labor intensive. A few highly trained professionals are needed. But a production force does not have to be more than semi-skilled, and in some cases can be unskilled.

Since this is a new area for most people we'd like to explore a few more examples of how cities might save money by using small-scale technology. Currently, sewage is a major problem in our cities. Municipal sewerage systems were usually designed and constructed during the early part of this century, and never were expected to handle current loads or to last this long. Many are in dire need of repair, yet this would require literally billions of dollars in municipal outlays. Treatment facilities are inadequate. Only one-half of our municipal treatment plants, according to the Federal Water Quality Control Board, are adequate. Drinking-water supplies now require a huge amount of chlorine to keep them purified, yet chlorine itself is in short supply. Coastal cities are finding that even the ocean cannot absorb the continuing deluge of billions of gallons of human waste. In New York City *raw sewage* is now within two miles of the shoreline and many experts predict that within two years it will be up on shore.

Yet there are simple, low-cost alternatives. In Washington, D.C., the authorities are spending hundreds of millions of dollars to modernize their treatment plant. By the time the new system is operational it will be overloaded, by the planners' own admission. They still haven't spent the money to separate the sanitary- and storm-sewer systems. Whenever it rains, the raw sewage is shunted directly into nearby Potomac River. However, a preliminary study indicates that, given the amount of money the city is willing to spend on modernizing treatment facilities, in-house, non-water-carrying disposal systems could be installed in almost every house in the District. This would conserve water, capture wastes to be used as fertilizer, and lead to the cleaning up of the Potomac River, with its major recreational potential.

One more example. The internal-combustion-engine car with its steel body and five thousand pounds of weight requires large factories, with enormous capital expenditures. The pollution from cars requires air-pollution-control boards, and devices on the mufflers of cars which in turn lead to less efficient gasoline utilization. The cars consume huge quantities of petroleum, and with the thousands of moving parts in an internal-combustion-engine car there are many repairs necessary, which increase the cost of the vehicle for its owners. The cars are noisy, bulky, and smelly. They are large, in size and horsepower, even though the average urban trip is less than two and a half miles and the average urban auto carries fewer than two people per trip.

Electric vehicles, on the other hand, with lightweight plastic bodies, can be manufactured in small factories, possibly located within a city. Electric motors can be made in very small shops. Plastic-injection-molding techniques reduce considerably the amount of capital needed to produce car bodies. The cars are quiet, and small. They require less energy to operate because when the accelerator is not depressed, the electrical connection is broken, thereby cutting off electricity from the batteries, whereas the fuel consumed while idling in internal-combustion vehicles represents a significant amount of the petroleum consumption in inner-city driving. Electric cars also have very few movable parts to go wrong and therefore save money on repairs.

So we have a choice. Nuclear-power plants, metropolitan sewage-treatment plants, internal-combustion engines or solar cells, in-house waste-cycling systems, and electric cars. It is not only an ecological and economic choice, but a deeply political one. It asks whether we want to move our productive facilities back into our communities, or remain at the mercy of isolated forces operating on criteria that give human concerns a low priority.

The Neighborhood's Carrying Capacity

We are entering a period of scarcity amid supposed affluence. The energy crisis, the various raw-materials shortages, rising food prices, are all interrelated. We are ending a period of rapid growth made possible by easily mined materials and cheap energy. In only a century we have burned most of the easily accessible fossil fuels; we have gobbled up a major part of our ores. Now we are entering a period when we will have to slow down our energy use, and our gross production of goods. This does not mean that we will have to lower our standard of living. Ironically, it might turn out that by lowering the quantity of goods we produce we can actually raise our standards of living.

Our Gross National Product measures not only production of goods, but production of "bads." It measures not only the production of cars, but the production of catalytic mufflers to eliminate the fumes from exhaust pipes, and it measures, as a product, the money spent to alleviate diseases and other human malfunctions caused by the fumes. It measures not only food production, but sewage-treatment plant production. Because it is only a gross statistic the GNP condones obsolescence, not durability. The quicker we run our goods down, or design them to break down, the better off we are, according to our gross-national-product figures. Common sense tells us that this is riddled with faulty logic.

We are moving into an era of what might be called a steady state economy. Interestingly enough, it is the ecologists who were the first to have coined the phrase. The economists, trained during an era of rapid growth and energy-intensive production, will probably be the last to change their thinking. A steady state economy does not mean that we have no progress, no changes, no advances. It does mean that those changes will have to be much more conscious, because we cannot continue to "waste" our resources on industries based upon fast obsolescence and rapid changes of style. It means that we will have to begin making choices between qualities as well as quantities of production. Industries already are having to make choices as to whether they will produce gasoline, vinyl chloride, chlorine, or petrochemical fertilizers, all coming from the same crude-oil base. This means, in a more concrete sense, that we are choosing whether to run our cars, drink our tap water (chlorine is used to purify water), listen to our choice of home music (polyvinyl chloride is used in record manufacturing), or eat abundant supplies of food (petrochemical fertilizers). We are suddenly faced with a reality in which we cannot do all these things as easily as in the past. Resources and energy are tighter.

One way of coming to terms with a steady state economy is to figure out what the carrying capacity of our land and our communities is. This is important for a number of reasons. It will tell us how much subsidy we are getting from Mother Nature. It will tell us how much we can rely on our own natural resources. And, perhaps most important of all, it can help us to redefine, or finally, understand our place as people in the natural world, and our place as a nation in the political world.

As the world enters an era of resource and energy scarcity, it might be easy for the United States to trim the fat off its production techniques, tighten its belt a little, and continue to import energy, raw materials, and even food from the rest of the world. But common sense tells us that sooner or later Americans will have to operate within a world energy and resource budget in which each country will demand an equitable share. On the neighborhood level we can begin to move in that direction now, and voluntarily, by actually estimating how much can be produced within the community, and how much subsidy is necessary to obtain things that can't be.

Carrying-capacity studies are extraordinarily complicated. The technique is still in its infant stages, and requires much refinement. Carrying-capacity studies have been done by Howard Odum, a professor at the University of Florida, in that state, and are being duplicated and refined in Oregon and Vermont. The following is not a scientific carrying-capacity study, but rather a first step toward estimating the neighborhood's natural-resource reserve, a way to take an inventory that can be useful.

Directory of Resources

Each neighborhood is different. Each has its own peculiar capacity and limitations. In some neighborhoods there might be a preponderance of people with manual skills. In others the majority might be unemployed. In some there could be wide expanses of land, in others empty warehouses, long growing seasons, windy environments. Some of these factors can be an asset as a neighborhood strives for self-sufficiency.

HUMAN RESOURCES

One way of starting to survey a neighborhood's resources is to begin with its human wealth, by going house-to-house, knocking on doors, getting to know the neighbors, finding out what skills they have, what tools or special equipment they possess, what facilities they have access to, what knowledge they possess. In one block in Washington, D.C., such a survey uncovered plumbers, electricians, engineers, amateur gardeners, lawyers, and teachers. In addition, a vast number of tools were discovered; complete workshops, incomplete machine-tool shops, and extended family relationships which added to the neighborhood's inventory — an uncle in the hardware business, an aunt in the cosmetics industry, a brother teaching biology downtown. The organizing of a directory of human resources can be an organizing tool itself. Possibly, if it is an outgrowth of a community hardware store, it can include a survey of broken items in the neighborhood. What services do people need most? What are the problems with most appliances? Are people willing to give a certain amount of money each year ($10, $20?) in order to have a group maintenance plan, with neighbors fixing appliances and gadgets and giving advice on redesigning houses for capturing more heat in the winter and cold air in the summer.

The checklist of professional and labor resources should be extended from households to institutions. If there are colleges and high schools in the area, find out when laboratories might be available for local use. See if there is computer time available (there often is), what tools and facilities there are. Vocational schools, of course, have complete tool shops for many purposes. Make an inventory of skills of the local college and public-school faculties. Who is a practicing attorney, an engineer, an artist, etc.?

This kind of inventory is readily available in any small town or rural area where everyone, having lived together through many crises, knows what each other's abilities are. In urban areas we need to conduct a census to determine what our neighbors do and what their skills are.

Often what our neighbor does is not as important as what he or she *can* do. The sociologist might be an expert plumber in his spare time; the housewife, an excellent gardener. The lawyer might be a fine flutist; the engineer a superb artist. Hobbies are often more telling, for the hobby is an avocation, chosen for pleasure, whereas an occupation is possibly chosen for prestige, money, or survival.

NATURAL RESOURCES

Natural resources can be broken down into subcategories, such as space, weather, wastes, food production.

Space. Go to your local zoning board or local library and get out a zoning map. It will tell you which neighborhood areas are zoned residential, commercial, industrial — and what subcategories there are. Sometimes by walking around the area you will discover space that had previously escaped your attention. Even warehouses may be inconspicuously hidden away in the recesses of a neighborhood. Get an aerial map of the community, available at the local land office, or go to the roof of the tallest building with a zoning map spread out to orient yourself. This will give you a bird's-eye view of rooftop space, and can also give you a preliminary glimpse of available sunlight and tree shade.

After surveying the neighborhood's space, break that space down into the following categories: soil space, rooftop space, recreation space (parks, playgrounds), street and alley space. The last two should be broken down still further in terms of which could conceivably be closed to vehicular traffic and used for something else.

In addition to outdoor space, survey the indoor space. Church basements are often vacant and available for community use. What about local schools after class hours? Public libraries? Theater auditoriums? Hospitals? Garages?

Weather Patterns. Investigate the average rainfall, total precipitation, number of freezing days, date of last frost, average year-round temperature. The rainfall can be an indication of how much water is available for drinking and washing if all ground sources became polluted or were cut off. The date of the last frost marks the time that vegetables can be set outside in the soil without protection. Keep in mind that because of the concrete in cities, which retains heat, and the warmth generated from auto exhausts, packed human bodies, and air conditioners, a city never gets quite as cold as the suburbs, so if your initial weather figures are standard weather-bureau observations at centers located outside the downtown area add ten degrees for inner-city temperature. But the weather-bureau figures cannot be as exact as readings you collect yourself right in the community.

Sunlight-availability information can be obtained from the weather office in most cities. They can tell you the average number of hours of sunlight in every month of the year, and this is a good figure to use later when estimating the quantity of vegetables which can be grown within the area. Finally, the weather bureau can give you insolation figures, the amount of sunlight that falls per square meter in your area. This can be useful in estimating energy output for the neighborhood.

Wastes. We can rapidly, though crudely, estimate the amount of human, organic, and trash wastes coming from a neighborhood. The sanitation department usually has a summary of the composition of refuse coming from the entire city. It might even have subunit breakdowns. The composition varies substantially from city to city. In Flint, Michigan, for example, in 1969, 17.5 percent of its mixed solid residuals were paper products and 32.6 percent were food wastes. In Alexandria, Virginia, on the other hand, a study done in 1968 found that almost 58 percent of its refuse was paper products and only 6 percent food wastes.

The refuse in a city is not in a literal sense a natural resource, because, for example, paper comes from trees and the trees do not grow in the neighborhood. But in the short term it can be used as a resource. Recycling is a way of diminishing the neighborhood's dependence on outside sources for raw materials. Some environmentalists have been telling people that their refuse is suddenly a "resource" because it can be burned to produce energy. It must be remembered, however, that every time we burn refuse, we then need to produce more refuse to be used as a "resource," which takes more energy and raw materials.

Human and organic waste, however, *is* a natural resource. The human body excretes a significant percentage of the food energy it takes in. Much of this energy is carried in urine and feces. These items are rich in minerals and energy. Urine contains urea, an important nitrogen base for fertilizer. It also contains potash. The average person in America produces around 65 pounds of dry waste each year. Given the mineral content of that waste, the average adult produces 7 pounds of phosphorus and 5 pounds of potash each year. If we multiply the number of people in the neighborhood by these figures we get a gross aggregate of fertilizer available for food production. This human waste (plus the other organic waste which we will talk about next) can also be used to produce methane gas, which in turn can be used as a fuel in cars or for heating and cooking.

In addition to the human wastes there are organic wastes in the neighborhood, such as food scraps, garden trimmings, grass cuttings, etc. The average person throws away about 225 pounds of vegetable waste per year. This can be added to the human wastes, speeding and enriching the fertilizer component as well as the methane generation.

To give you a rough idea of what waste might yield, we can take a brief look at Littleton, Colorado, where there is a sewage-treatment system for a town of 40,000 inhabitants, roughly equal to the population of many inner-city neighborhoods. Littleton has both methane digestion systems and flat areas for fertilizer drying beds. It generates, from the population of 40,000 people, the equivalent of 250 gallons of gasoline per day and hundreds of cubic yards of high-quality fertilizer. If we have lightweight vehicles, which can get up to 25 miles per gallon, that amount of methane could give about 6,300 miles per day of transportation (with much less air pollution than is the case with burning gasoline). This is an enormous amount of travel when we consider that the neighborhood in question might be no more than one or two square miles in area.

Soil and Water. After estimating the fertilizer resources of the community it is important to test the soil and water to find out what minerals it has and which it lacks. This is important for water in that it can help determine what kind of nutrients are needed when growing vegetables in non-soil environments (discussed more fully below). The soil samples will tell what extra minerals might be added besides the fertilizer generated from the community. Soil and water analyses will be done free of charge by local county extension or water offices.

Food Production

You have already done part of the work by exploring the space availability in the neighborhood and the sunlight and fertilizer potential. Now we should look at the vegetable and protein yields.

Vegetable. This gets us into the murky area of human nutrition and basic needs. It is not enough to examine how much of each food item could be raised in a given geographic area. It must be seen how far the neighborhood can go in producing a *balanced* diet, protein, minerals, vitamins, fats, carbohydrates, and fibers.

The content of the food we eat can vary markedly, depending on whether the vegetable or grain has been grown in good or bad soil and whether it has been harvested at the right time and prepared properly. Thus, any analysis you will undertake will have to take into account a considerable number of factors.

Department of Agriculture technicians use the rough rule of thumb that to feed one American one acre of land is needed. Other studies indicate that we might get by with less. One researcher in California has preliminary figures indicating that one-eighth of an acre might be enough to feed one person on a vegetarian diet for a year. Whatever projections, there are some hard data available on current yields of various crops. The extension agent, once again, will give you yields for your area of the country. These yields may be conservative, for there have been numerous advances in small-scale intensive agriculture. In Palo Alto and Santa Clara, California, people are investigating a technique of labor-intensive gardening called biodynamic gardening. In some areas, scientific advances in cross-planting various vegetables for space-saving purposes are being integrated into family plots. And, finally, and maybe most exciting for inner-city areas, there are the possibilities of greenhouse techniques, using soil or other media as the base.

Hydroponics is a method by which plants are grown in media other than soil, with nutrients provided periodically in solution. It is not a new technique. Some forty percent of the tomatoes sold in Phoenix, Arizona, for example, come from hydroponic greenhouses. The importance of this technique is threefold. First, yields seem to be higher than with soil gardening. In fact, preliminary calculations based on data from NASA and commercial growers, suggest that if two percent of the area of a city (a fraction of its rooftop space) could be used for rooftop greenhouses, the vegetable needs of at least 10,000 people per square mile, a figure near the average density in American cities, could be supplied year round. Second, it prevents the depletion of soil which is so scarce in the city. Third, soil might well be too heavy on residential rooftops. But soil-less media, such as a combination of perlite and vermiculite or small clay pellets, are quite light.

Now take the space in soil that you have, the rooftop space, the streets or alleys that might be closed off, the vacant lots, and the yards. Estimate what number of hours of sunlight these get during the growing season (some front yards might be shady throughout the year, which means they could be used to grow certain crops needing less direct sunlight, like cabbages). Then estimate how much fertilizer you can reclaim and what its composition is. Integrating all this information can give you a rough idea of the food-carrying capability of your tiny nation, your neighborhood.

Protein. People don't live by vegetables alone. Although, as we shall note, we can get some protein from vegetables (some say all), it is not at all clear that people will forsake meat or fish unless they are on the verge of starvation. The average person needs .9 grams of protein per kilogram of weight. This means that a 150 pound person would need 3 ounces. Get a census for your neighborhood. It breaks down the population into age groups.

Then get a weight chart for each age group. This will give you a method for roughly estimating how much protein your neighborhood needs to survive.

Meat is not the only source of protein. Other foods compare favorably with meat. Part of the reason is that it is not only the quantity but the quality of our protein intake which is important. Protein needs certain combinations of amino acids in order to be utilized efficiently by the body. In other words, one food might have more protein quantity, but because of its combination of amino acids, less of it is used in the body per weight than another food. In her well-known book *Diet for a Small Planet*, Frances Moore Lappe gives a chart concerning the Net Protein Utilization (NPU).

Some of the best sources of protein are fish and eggs, meat and soybeans. Although there may be municipal ordinances which prohibit the raising of some fowl and animals within the city limits, it is a good idea to estimate what kind of production you can get in any case. Some sources of protein, like cattle, are ruled out in the beginning. It takes more than twenty pounds of cereal protein to produce one pound of beef protein, an inefficiency Americans have lived with for many years, much to the detriment of the rest of the world which has seen its level of arable land for human-use cereal production reduced while it raises beef cattle for export. It takes six pounds of cereal protein to get one pound of hog meat, and two and a half pounds of vegetable protein fed to our chickens to get one pound of animal protein in return.

There are interesting compromises which are possible for those who eat meat. Chickens, for example, can survive on a diet of flies, and some people in Palo Alto are currently devising an effective fly trap for just this purpose. Rabbits can survive on scraps, and, of course, their rate of reproduction is legendary.

Fish are good converters of protein. Rainbow trout, for example, produce 16 ounces of fish flesh for every 24 ounces of feed they eat. What is more, they can be raised intensively in very small areas, even in urban basements. Experiments are now in progress around the country involving lobster cultivation and shrimp, salmon, catfish, and trout rearing. Lobster and shrimp research is still in the preliminary stages — in any event, lobster research is being done because of the high cost per pound, with a view to the commercial market, rather than as a low-cost way to bring food to millions of undernourished people. Recent investigations in California with shrimp, however, have tentatively found that this omnivorous animal can be fed a diet of vegetables and scraps, rather than meat, and still thrive. Rapid advances are being made in salmon research in Providence, Rhode Island, and in closed loop catfish farming in Woods Hole, Massachusetts. In Providence, there is the report that salmon grow to 2 pounds in 18 months in fresh-water tanks, and then grow rapidly to 8 pounds in salt water facilities. In Washington, D.C., Dr. Fern Wood Mitchell has raised fish eggs to maturity in his basement, using a simple tank and filter system, using city water in very small quantities (25 gallons per day compared with 25 gallons per minute in traditional commercial trout farming). In Milheim, Pennsylvania, Marine Protein Company has now begun to raise 2,000,000 pounds of trout per surface acre, more than 150 times what had been the average figure in outdoor fish ponds before. The fish are raised in 12-by-17-foot food silos.

There are possible interlocks between these systems. For example, rainbow trout are especially good for urban areas because they can be raised intensively. But, they have two drawbacks. They require high-grade protein (usually fish meal) as a diet, and they require cold water. Energy must be used to keep their space air-conditioned. It may be possible to use windmills to generate the electricity for the air-conditioning (see the section on energy below). Or one can look to other types of fish. One group in Woods Hole, Massachusetts, is working with Tilapia, a kind of catfish, which is a warm-water fish and herbivorous (it does not require meat to survive). Several people around the world are currently experimenting with systems by which human waste can be used to raise algae, a simple-celled plant organism, which can in turn be fed to fish in indoor tanks. The more ways that the system of food production, consumption, waste can be closed, the more a neighborhood can become independent of outside sources of energy and food.

Energy Generation

Almost all of our energy comes from the sun. Green plants use sunlight to produce energy through the process of photosynthesis. We have access to that energy when we eat the plants. Over millions of years a tiny fraction of the plants decay and are compressed under tremendous pressures to form the concentrated forms of energy called fossil fuels. Contemporary civilization has been built on fossil fuels because, until recently, it has been relatively easy to tap the enormous concentrations of energy contained in these fuels.

However, solar energy comes in many other forms. The sun heats up the atmosphere to different degrees in different areas, causing winds, which can be harnessed by various wind devices. The sun evaporates water, which then falls as rain on land areas, running off to form rivers which can be harnessed to get hydroelectric power. The sun's heat can be captured directly to heat homes, dry produce, and even cool things. And, finally, the sun's energies can be used to produce electricity directly via the use of a device called a photovoltaic cell.

We would be lucky, indeed, to live in a neighborhood that had its own oil well. But every neighborhood has its share of sunlight, and every community is swept by the wind. These alternate sources of energy can fulfill a significant percentage of the community's energy needs. They are, however, diffuse forms of energy, requiring a great deal of space in order to get a significant amount of energy. But it seems probable that very shortly we can support many of our necessary neighborhood activities through other than fossil fuel energy.

The technologies for capturing these various forms of energy and converting them to useful work are in different stages of development. Solar collectors for space and water heating are well-developed, already competitive with fossil-fuel home heating, and easily available. Their main drawback is that existing structures may require major structural alterations to achieve maximum use of solar collectors.

Windmills are also technically advancing. But there are engineering problems associated with maintenance, output in low winds, and storage capacity.

Photovoltaic cells still require technological breakthroughs, but these are coming so quickly that some predict that within fifteen years they too will be within range of the economics of fossil-fuel energy generation.

The local weather bureau should have insolation data for your region. This is pretty accurate. It also has wind maps, but these are somewhat less useful. The reason is that wind varies considerably in cities. A city would probably be less windy than a suburb because of the office buildings which cut down the wind. On the other hand, the tops of buildings might be more windy because of their altitude. There can be downdrafts in a city because of the tunnel-like environment between high-rise buildings. The only way to measure these elements accurately is to get an anemometer (wind-measuring device) and put it in different spots in the neighborhood. This would take many years to be totally accurate, but a few months can tell what the variation, if any, is from the local weather maps, which are usually recorded at suburban airports.

One thing to remember when estimating the energy that flows through the neighborhood: the efficiencies of devices that convert this energy into useful work is very low. For photovoltaic cells it hovers around 10 percent. For windmills it is a little higher. For solar collectors a little higher still. The efficiencies of many of these devices will increase with more research and experimentation, but it will never rise above 20 percent for solar cells nor 30–40 percent for windmills. Thus you should not total the amount of solar energy falling on the community and assume that is the amount that is usable to heat your home, light your workshop, or run your power tools.

Demonstration Models

The research into the carrying capacity of the neighborhood will not inevitably be transformed into community action. No matter how much information you compile about community resources, it is only when residents can see the results of such labors — can eat the tomatoes, taste the fish, see the gardens growing, watch the windmills spinning, feel the hot water heated by a solar collector — that they can relate to the visions that the research projects. Therefore, the next stage is to construct demonstration projects. Make a fish tank and stock it; put up several greenhouses and invite people to see how vegetables grow during the colder months; raise some vegetables hydroponically and sell them in community stores, with signs telling how they were grown; erect a windmill or two and show people how it generates electricity; buy a couple of solar cells and show residents how they can be used to power a transistor radio.

Demonstration models are an ideal way to create a link with those interested in these projects as a hobby and those interested in the economic possibilities. It is a way to attract the attention of different kinds of skilled people, from plumbers to bankers. It is a way to get publicity from city-wide news media. And it is a way to get in touch with people in the area who may have vital information or have demonstration models of their own, but did not know of what was going on in that tiny area of the city. In Washington, D.C., a group called Community Technology operates out of a warehouse in a low-income neighborhood. The warehouse has a fairly complete machine-tool shop and staff who can teach residents, young and old, how to handle various equipment. The community was at first curious about the goings-on in the warehouse. Then they began to make requests. The welding skills of one member were in high demand, building a bike rack in front of one food store, constructing a basketball hoop and backboard for youngsters across the street. Eventually kids wandered in to learn how to saw a board or handle a drill. Finally the combination of demonstration models and the availability of tools and a friendly and competent staff began to make its mark. Neighbors joined in building projects. Local colleges extended their personnel and equipment to this outreach post in the community. And people suddenly began talking about what "we did" and what "we can do."

Neighborhood Industry

Researching the carrying capacity of a neighborhood or proving that the economies of scale of many industries occur on the local level does not produce jobs or create wealth. But it does create a mood, an awareness of the potential for internally generated commerce. It creates a base of data and a direction, both of which can become important both in the neighborhood and the city itself.

Most cities are currently involved in the game called "attract the industrialist." Cities need to have productive facilities within their borders both to increase the employment rolls and to raise the tax base which in turn can underwrite public expenditures. The need is genuine, but the conclusion, that one must go far outside the area to attract business, is questionable. First, if the city does manage to attract industry, it has little control over it. The industry, if it is large (and the larger the better from the city's point of view), can become a fiefdom within the city and a major force in the local political system. It can pick up and leave at any time, even on a moment's notice. And, as noted before, if it is part of a national or multinational network, the facilities in one area are relatively unimportant and can be closed down when the profit picture in another area is rosier. Second, in order to attract industry a city must offer something. The offer might range from outlawing unions, to providing free public services, to lowering the tax assessment on its facilities. In Gary, Indiana, as recent studies have shown, United States Steel is subsidized by every taxpayer in that city for its pollution. Finally, every city is involved in the same game. Everyone competes with everyone else, offering up a table full of goodies to attract the few industries willing to listen. Not every city or town or neighborhood is lucky and rewarded for its efforts. When one wins, even in an economy that is growing rapidly, as in the late 1960s, it is most often the case that another loses.

A sense of self-reliance, on the other hand, could lead to the establishment of local industries. City officials, impressed by the evidence of a lack of economies of scale above the small-plant level, attracted to the idea of industry under the combined control of its workers and the community, and desiring to produce as many stable jobs as possible, could use municipal funds for investment purposes. One first step might be for the neighborhood to establish a community development corporation and contract with the city to provide basic services in the community. Most service operations are optimally run on the neighborhood level anyway, as the following chart shows. (These data, of course, use only per-capita-tax cost as their criterion. The quality and extent of services must also be taken into consideration, but recent studies are increasingly supporting the view that locally run service facilities are not only cost-effective, but produce better quality and more effective services.)

PER CAPITA COSTS OF SERVICES*

Population category

	Less than 10,000	*50,000 to 99,999*	*250,000 or more*
Police protection	$5.70	$7.50	$19.10
Fire Protection	1.42	4.85	10.81
Sewerage	2.65	6.30	10.61

* From *Statistical Abstract of the United States* for 1971, Tables 632 and 634, including data from Table 2.

The chart is, of course, general. In one city neighborhood, however, residents did their own study and discovered that it was costing the city between $60–80 for each ton of garbage which was picked up and disposed. A neighborhood church group found that it could set up its own recycling center in the community, contract with a buyer in the suburbs, recycle about 70 percent of the ordinary trash that people throw away, and get paid between $20–50 per ton, depending on the composition of the trash. Thus instead of the people of the city, through their taxes, paying *out* $60–80 enterprising neighbors were *getting* $20–50, a difference of $80–130 per ton, or hundreds of thousands of dollars if generalized to the entire city.

A possible next step, after contracting for providing neighborhood services, might be to establish manufacturing facilities. This is a most difficult step. It is difficult because small businesses have a failure rate of ninety percent in this country and this is as true in the processing or manufacturing sector or assembly sector as any other. While it is true that the economies of scale occur at relatively low production levels, it is also true that it is hard to break into distribution and marketing networks, so that production facilities, no matter how efficient, depend on a marketing system which does necessitate large-scale systems.

Some insightful studies have been done on community industries at the Center for Community Economic Development, located in Cambridge, Massachusetts. In one such study, by Mel Epstein and Thomas J. Shields, various growth industries were surveyed for their potential for community development corporations, including home-sewing supplies, microfiche and micropublishing, cable TV, limited-dividend housing, and minicomputers. Each is discussed in detail, including the amount of entry capital required and the kind of skills each might teach neighborhood residents. Some industries, such as limited-dividend housing or cable TV, require much more capital for entry than do others like microfilm or home-sewing supplies. The new-technology industries, like minicomputers and calculators, require fairly small amounts of capital for entry but the field is changing so rapidly that no neighborhood corporation could compete with the rapid entry of more efficient and cheaper products on the market. (The electronics industry is one of the few areas of our economy where technological advances are quickly incorporated and progress does mean better products; not coincidentally it is precisely in this field that there is a great deal of competition and the competitors are relatively small.)

Barry Stein, cited at length before in this chapter, after an exhaustive discussion of community corporations and their effect on the local economy, concluded that community enterprises should focus on consumer goods, rather than intermediate or producer goods, because they can undercut large corporations fairly easily, and the public relates directly to consumer firms, rather than to producer factories, so there is a much better chance to educate the community and gain its support. Stein also suggested that the production of basic industrial raw materials, like steel, sulfuric acid, and plastic resins, might not be effectively carried out in small highly decentralized plants. He proposed instead concentration upon the conversion, combination, and modification of such products to meet the final market demand.

The Agency for International Development has discussed the possibilities of small-scale industry for underdeveloped countries (which, after all, our neighborhoods are), listing the capital investment per employee and the number of employees that various industries would require. The data are reproduced below:

Industry	Capital investment/employee	Number of employees
Baking powder	$3200–5200	4–20
Apparel	$ 600–2600	20–40
Wooden furniture	$1600–6200	10–50
Thermosetting (plastic bowls)	$1700	20
Reinforced plastic molding (fiberglass sinks, chairs, etc.)	$4,000–8000	8–12

When choosing any industry it is important to differentiate the criteria used in community corporations as opposed to those used in commercial firms. As Epstein and Shields note, a commercial firm can generally take market prices as a given. It tries to operate so as to maximize its profit. This means maximizing the present value of future financial benefits. Each project is analyzed individually. The amount of investment and expected profit in each year in the future are detailed. It continues to borrow money and invest in projects until the market cost of capital to the firm equals the rate of return on the project.

However, community development corporations are not trying to maximize profits, but to maximize the well-being of the residents of the community. They therefore have multiple goals, which usually include:

— raising the material standard of living of residents in its community
— increasing the political and social power of the community in the wider society
— increasing the skill level of the residents
— increasing the sense of community and the quality of life within it.

As Epstein and Shields note, "Clearly, market prices have little meaning for a CDC in relation to most of these goals. The market does not reward the CDC for training workers or building political and organizational strength in a community."

By the time these questions arise in the neighborhood there will ideally be a strong assembly government where such ideas can be discussed. An assembly might vote its support to a particular industry opening up even though its prices are slightly higher because of the benefits gained by the community as a whole in higher employment, a greater degree of accountability by the business to the neighborhood, a higher quality product, and a sense of community responsibility. Questions of price, profit, and quality, and the related ones of growth, obsolescence, and needs, will probably occupy a great deal of time and energy during this stage in any community's development.

It is best, perhaps, to move gradually from one step in the production process to another. A bicycle collective might be established on the retail level. Then maintenance facilities might be added. After a number of people have learned the skills in repairs in a neighborhood, a factory could be initiated to produce a few vital parts, like chains or wheels or tires. Finally, if the need arises, full-scale production of bicycles could be attempted.

In the food sector we might start with the retail collectives, then add trucking distribution networks and warehouse storage areas. Later some food could be raised directly in the community. A canning factory might be set up to teach people to gain the advantage of low-priced fruits and vegetables in season all year round, by buying during the summer and eating during the winter. Finally, a glass recycling unit might be set up, at first to trade broken bottles for usable jars on an arrangement with the bottling companies, later possibly to produce the jars themselves.

At each of these steps, of course, the economics must be carefully examined. Division of labor between neighborhoods is not at all ruled out. One neighborhood might have a canning facility while another has more public space for vegetable gardening. Such divisions are beneficial and natural because they begin to hook neighborhoods together into a mutually supportive network.

Neighborhoods, as we have tried to make clear throughout this book, are not only the basic social unit for any nation but can also become productive, self-governing units to a very great extent. Before the reader raises the question of neighborhood parochialism and small-town isolationism and prejudice, however, we hasten to add that as neighborhoods gain a sense of self-confidence and self-awareness, they will become much more outward-oriented, much more than ever before. Checkpoint-Charlies on a neighborhood's borders seem unlikely (although it is interesting to note in this connection that many cities have recently passed laws barring further immigration into their areas: one city in Florida went so far as to pass a law — later reversed — asking the last 25,000 of its residents to move out!). As people begin to look to their own resources for the answers to pressing problems, and discover that local wisdom and creativity is often as good and certainly more pertinent than national planners' and experts' reports, they will be even more eager to communicate with like-minded communities and individuals. Neighbor Power and Neighborhood Cooperation are but opposite sides of the same coin.

EIGHT

Intercommunalism:
Neighborhood Cooperation

As the neighborhood moves through the various stages of development, two complementary movements occur, equally important. In one sense the community begins to move inward, trying to push the limits of its self-sufficiency, trying to see how many of its basic needs can be satisfied within its borders. New social arrangements are formed; new economic institutions are established. The neighborhood tries to develop mechanisms for controlling its territory and wealth, and then looks to ways to produce its goods and services with native industry and resources.

In the food sector warehouses are established, and then processing plants, flour mills, bakeries. People begin to investigate the land and rooftop and indoor space available within the area to see how much produce and protein can be raised within the neighborhood. A checklist of resources is begun, including a directory of skills, equipment, and space, as well as an investigation of the potential of natural resources like wind, water, sun, and human wastes. People are beginning to explore new technologies appropriate to neighborhood production. Intensive fish rearing, hydroponics, utilization of human and organic wastes, biodynamic farming, electronic microminiaturization, small metal and plastic plants, all undergo close scrutiny as the neighborhood directs its attention and energy inward, examining its potential.

News is redefined as events, ideas, opinions, and knowledge

which is generated in the neighborhood and/or is useful or of interest to its residents. Wall posters, newsletters, videotapes, newspapers, minicomputers, all lend support to a social cohesion which has become increasingly geographically based. The neighborhood assembly or government is beginning to symbolize this cohesion, and represents the community in its dealings with the city. Lines of communication between neighborhood and city are becoming two-way. Neighborhood corporations are negotiating with the city to take over service operations on a contractual basis for the neighborhood; legislation has been designed to devolve tax revenue and some legislative power to the neighborhood. Creative suggestions, and some informal working models concerning neighborhood security forces and local courts have been discussed or implemented.

In other words, this period of development has been, for the most part, inward-oriented, even parochial in its direction. There have been political points made, to be sure, and education has developed parallel to institution building. The concepts of workers' collectives, of surplus capital, of consumerism, of absentee land ownership, of racism and sexism, of age prejudice, of community justice, of self-taxation, of citizenship, have all been more clearly defined and explored. Although the neighborhood is still not entirely unified, those who are old-timers and those who are newcomers are beginning to work together as each recognizes the other's skills and experience and usefulness.

There is, however, another dynamic at work, one that becomes increasingly powerful as time goes by. That is an outward movement, interconnecting many communities in the cities and even the world. It is a natural and almost inevitable tendency. While there are many who try to build citizenship into the neighborhood itself, there are others who try to build strong links among many communities, reinforcing each other in their struggles. This outward movement occurs on a number of levels. The food collectives might establish a trucking cooperative to link medium and small farms with the warehouse operation in the city. As the truckers branch out in wider circles, they begin to form the basis for communications, and even trade, among regions. Trucks from Washington, D.C., for example, can move up to Boston and over to Pittsburgh and back, forming a regional network within which many neighborhoods fit. In and around Minneapolis there are already the beginnings of a delivery network, starting with food, that stretches across the Midwest. Even within a city interneighborhood trade patterns begin to reorient thinking, forcing us to think about balance of payments, rates of exchange, and new kinds of interdependence.

The intercommunal movement occurs partially as a natural outgrowth from an expanding economic base, but also because the neighborhood's residents at this point in its development begin to understand the limitations of the underdeveloped-nation model as an analogy to their own situation. They begin to feel the lack of political power, the frustration of constantly dealing with narrow and petty bureaucrats, and, especially, the feeling of being one small piece in a complex international economic system governed by very powerful forces.

Often the first inter-links occur as a result of one neighborhood's fight against one large corporation. Just as labor unions, decades ago, began to link up with each other to combat a national corporation, so neighborhoods begin to do the same thing. A case in point occurred in Washington, D.C., when a fast-food operation — Gino's — attempted to move into one neighborhood. T-shirts were quickly printed, decrying *Ginocide*, petitions were signed, court suits were initiated against the restaurant as a possible public nuisance. The stockholders' meeting in another town was picketed and business officials were cornered. But one of the most powerful and effective weapons was the solidarity that was building between this neighborhood and others. Gino's operations in other parts of Washington, in Virginia, and even in New York City, were picketed and boycotted. The managers of those franchises began to pressure the company to drop its plans for expansion into the D.C. neighborhood, which it promptly did.

Such cooperation becomes important as the community begins to see the difference between mobilizing widespread support in pickets, petitions, demonstrations, block parties, and boycotts, as opposed to trying to fight such a move in the zoning commission, or the local courts. The latter blurs the issue, causing the community to rely on the judgment of one judge or group of judges. Since there is no ongoing pressure, the legal question becomes the overriding one. There are many problems with this, but the primary one is that the legal system is not designed to stop the encroachment of outside interests into the neighborhood. It was never meant to, and only the most clever lawyer could win a case on these points. These cases are more often than not argued on technicalities, and even if there is a victory, it is a tenuous and probably temporary one. On the other hand, businesses and industries are quite vulnerable to being whipsawed. This is a maneuver, used by labor unions in their early days, of picketing one business and asking people to do their shopping at other businesses, even though the other one is no better than the one being picketed. Thus, for example, one might picket Gino's and ask people interested in fast-food outlets to patronize McDonalds, or vice versa. Many people interested in hamburgers and French fries might not be political enough to join a picket line, but neither are they interested in crossing one if they need only walk down the street to get what they want. This is why a multi-city, multi-neighborhood action against companies can prove much more effective than an interminable lawsuit.

It is important, however, not to overuse or misuse the tactic. This is what ideological purists do, boycotting almost everything under the sun, and thereby making a fine moral point, but an indefensible tactical one. Boycotting the products of all companies which are linked to foreign wars is probably impossible; boycotting one company is not.

Thus the movement outward develops naturally, from a need for mutual defense against economic institutions much larger than one neighborhood, and from a need for trade and communications with like-minded communities. There are good theoretical reasons for linking up with neighborhoods and cities around the world. But the reasons are not immediately compelling. In fact, seeking such links might produce tensions within the neighborhood itself. Yet, in the long run, cooperation with neighborhoods and cities in other parts of the world may be the only way to support political struggles against multinational corporations, and such cooperation is needed as a mechanism to fight American parochialism, commercial imperialism, and arrogance with respect to our role in the world.

As the neighborhood, or neighborhoods, actually become effective political units — as they begin to attain an image as actually threatening to corporate profits, or entrenched political interests, or real-estate developers, or rich people — very powerful machinery of the state and its allies will be brought to bear on the tiny community. This might come on the bureaucratic level first. Housing inspectors may begin to investigate housing, citing obscure and not-so-obscure sanitary regulations. Health inspectors may begin to give community food stores or restaurants low scores on their reports, forcing investments in new machinery. Police may begin to survey the community very closely, making marijuana arrests, stopping cars, hassling drivers and pedestrians alike. This is the lowest level of harassment and the most common. If the neighborhood has made allies within the city bureaucracy and can deliver votes at election time, it can usually postpone these pressures until it gets on its feet. But — and it is important not to forget — this can only be postponed *until* the neighborhood gets on its feet. As it begins to sever its relations with major economic interests, and builds its own wealth, the votes it delivers may not be as important as the money that the economic interests can deliver in the municipal arena. As this begins to happen, the neighborhood must move in two directions to defend itself. The first, and most natural arena, is that of municipal politics. The second is national and international cooperation and intercommunication with other neighborhoods.

Entering Municipal Politics

The entrance into municipal politics can occur on two, somewhat contradictory, levels. The first is to gain power in order to decentralize power. This means campaigning on a platform to give authority and power back to the neighborhoods. This, of course, is the classic problem of politics. How do we gain power in order to give it up? Is the dynamic of gaining power itself self-corrupting? Will we decide that one group can wield that power much more effectively than can an entire neighborhood composed of conflicting ideologies and prejudices and opinions? The road to power has been walked by many well-intentioned people who thought that once there, they could decentralize the operations of office.

One way to deal with this problem is to have a clear program when running for office. This should not be difficult, for much of the research and activities done over the previous several years in neighborhood development can be useful in designing such a program. People must be clear as to what, if any, powers should be left to the cities; where service operations should be decentralized; how budgetary items could be decentralized. Also, any campaign must run on a platform, not on personal appeal or individual good looks. That helps prevent the kind of egoism that leads to arrogance and cult-of-personality leadership.

It is also important, however, to understand and deal with the question of leadership on the municipal level. We have previously discussed the nature of problems inherent in neighborhood leadership and neighborhood government, the problems of representation versus assembly government, and of decision making on the local level. These problems are magnified on the municipal level and become worse because there is ready-made power available on that level and the people are separated by a great distance, both physical and cultural, from their representatives. These are very difficult questions to deal with, and each neighborhood and city will have to decide for itself what its priorities are. In Wisconsin, for example, the Wisconsin Alliance Party had many internal discussions as to the nature of political leadership. At one time it was thought by many that if the people in one's constituency were opposed to their representative's vote, it was his or her duty to resign. It was felt that this would teach people that they and their opinions are worthwhile. Also, and probably more important, the representative was felt to have been doing a poor job of educating his or her constituency if they did not agree with the issues as presented. This is the critical difference between a new kind of politics and the old one. Power is won in order to educate people and give them the room they need to develop their unique directions. In America's traditional politics, there is usually only one goal after winning the election — winning the next one.

One reason for entering municipal politics is to win breathing room for the neighborhood. It is a way to give the neighborhood zoning powers, service contracts, a way to reorient tax revenues, redefine education, give control of the police back to the communities. It is a natural extension of neighborhood self-defense and a powerful tool in its own right.

But another reason to move into the municipal political arena is to have a stronger base from which to deal with the powerful institutions which affect neighborhood life. The neighborhood sustaining fund is important in order to educate people from the ground up, and marks the beginning of a sense of domestic capital. But questions of surplus capital can only be tackled adequately on a city level. At that level there are huge pension funds as well as tax-exempt bonding power which can be utilized, tax rates which can be changed. Winning power in the municipal government means winning some control of the city's educational system, and its police force, and its legal talent. It provides numerous opportunities for defense, and for self-sufficiency. Although the neighborhood is the human and social base for a new society, the city is a first-stage basic political and legal base to safeguard the interests of the embryonic nation. Above everything else there is the simple truth that the city government *does* exist and *is* the one closest to a neighborhood.

The first and the second reasons can conflict and can provide the fuel for much internal discussion. The first talks of giving up power, the second of enhancing it. Unfortunately, life is not as simplistic as we would like it to be, and this contradiction must be accepted for a time. In the long run a new society can be built only from the bottom up, by educating people into a new value system, by giving people a sense of self-confidence, by allowing people to develop their own uniqueness. In the short run very powerful interests oppose these tendencies and must be kept at bay as much as possible. In the long run neighborhoods can become ecological systems, moving toward self-reliance in many areas. In the short run one has to deal with Consolidated Edison,

AT&T, General Motors. In the short run one has to think in terms of municipalizing the uitility companies, or starting public telephone systems, or publicly owned and operated manufacturing systems. It is on a municipal level that many of these ideas can be concretely realized in the immediate future.

Still, even cities are not invulnerable to outside pressure. A small city in South Dakota, several years ago, used its powers of eminent domain to take over its electric company. This occurred on the retail level. The same company retained ownership of the generating facilities and transmission lines. It refused to bring in electricity over its lines, and the city went to court. The Supreme Court, in a four to three decision, supported the city. In Georgia the utility companies almost railroaded through the state legislature a bill which would have prohibited cities from establishing publicly owned power campanies. There are numerous examples from the last century of states' withdrawing powers from municipalities when these cities exercised these powers against major economic interests. A late nineteenth-century Supreme Court verdict, the Dillon decision, ruled that cities were, in fact, mere creatures of their states, and could even be eliminated as legal entities whenever the state saw fit.

Yet cities are far different from neighborhoods in their power. The mayor of that small city in South Dakota could certainly have mobilized strong citizen action if the electric company had won its lawsuit. Cities can, and have, gained control over their electric companies in many cases, and most recently cities are themselves forming buying clubs to own and purchase energy directly from the source. Cities could, theoretically, prohibit internal-combustion-engine cars on their streets and manufacture electric cars in neighborhood assembly plants, cars which could only be rented, not purchased. It is almost one hundred years since the Dillon decision declared that cities existed at the mere whim of the states; it is difficult to believe that a city's powers could be stripped from it so easily anymore.

Once cities begin to move against national economic or political interests, however, they too will be caught up in the sort of dilemma that neighborhoods face, one of tackling organizations infinitely more powerful than themselves. It is possible, of course, to extrapolate the above discussion and ask that the cities of a state move toward state power, but we think that would be inappropriate. The reasons are that this kind of power, although very much greater and less vulnerable than that of cities (no court has yet said that states were a mere creation of the federal government, although they are moving in that direction), is remote from citizen participation. Cities could, however, move into the state political arena to *decentralize* some state power, giving it to the cities themselves, and have done so in certain areas of the country, particularly in Pennsylvania.

Rather than continually moving up the political ladder, we suggest that cities have quite enough resources to deal with most issues, and that they should begin interconnecting with other cities, just as neighborhoods have done, when they are fighting major interest groups. Cities do have the wherewithal to develop their own worldwide communications networks. They can develop their own industries, and work in association with other cities around the world when their interests are threatened by multinational corporations.

Here we have been discussing power, but now we must talk about that most abstract of things, morality. We are now residents of the richest country in the history of the world. Most of this wealth did not come as a result of our own sweat and industry, but as a result of our blessedly rich topsoil, and natural resources; our wealth of space, and isolation from foreign wars. These created the foundations for the industrial system which in turn has given us our newly gained technological wealth. Furthermore, a significant portion of our wealth has been gained at the expense of peoples around the world. We have kept our access to cheap energy open by heavy-handed financial policies. Cheap raw materials have been assured by political interventions and military counterinsurgency techniques. Bananas are cheap in American markets, partially because Guatemalan workers are not unionized and are paid very low wages. American products are being increasingly manufactured abroad, lowering their cost, but producing huge economic and social inequities in the underdeveloped world's labor force. Americans eat more than their share of meat, causing lower protein consumption in those countries of the world where vast acreage is shifted over to meat production for export rather than cereal production for domestic consumption.

This does not mean that any neighborhood movement, even a wealthy American one, should operate out of guilt. No viable movement can do so, nor should it. The fact that our unique natural resources combined with the talent of our immigrants have given us this wealth should not embarrass us. But it means taking care that localism and neighborhood control do not quickly degenerate into isolationism and elitism. Fortress America is impossible in any case, but to focus on such an image while multinational corporations vend their wars and ways in Taiwan, Chile, and Brazil is a poor vision indeed. We must begin to link up with neighborhoods of the world in order to learn their problems, and share our resources. We must export our surplus, not consume it ourselves in waste and style.

One way of avoiding this is to stick with the checklist of neighborhood resources mentioned in the last chapter. By relying primarily on those resources available in the neighborhood, that is, its wind, sun, waste products, soil, ingenuity, professional resources, etc., we can become ecological in our living patterns and not live off the rest of the world. And even here we have a tremendous head start. We have great technological talent, modern machinery, fine laboratories, relatively cheap and good equipment, millions of educated people, good communications systems, and wide, open spaces.

Developing Intercommunal Links

From this base we can establish intercommunal links with other countries, villages, neighborhoods, or communes, to begin a dialogue about mutual needs and support. On a domestic scale this outreach might grow out of trade patterns. Trucking cooperatives might begin to make contractual arrangements with co-op food producers in other parts of the region to buy their food in bulk, store it at a central warehouse, and distribute it through buying clubs, collectives, or local, sympathetic businesses. Arrangements could be made with federations of small farmers to pick up their produce on a regular schedule.

The next step could be to make the trade two-way, bringing into the network those towns and villages in between the major trading points. Trucks could take fish raised in Washington, D.C., to a rural town in Appalachia and exchange this for coal. The exchange of high-quality protein for high-quality energy could be arranged through a contract between the United Mine Workers and a District neighborhood corporation.

These economic links should be combined with communication links. A coal miners' strike can be supported by urban dwellers and vice versa. We need to develop communication so that people get an understanding of each other's needs. Otherwise the trading economy will quickly and easily degenerate into the same competitive and mutual distrust patterns that currently characterize most trading patterns. New systems of exchange could be established, breaking away from the international monetary system, with its artificial constructs. A currency might be based on a range of commodities, as suggested by economist Ralph Borsodi. Or one could be based on labor units, or energy units, or time units, as suggested by earlier American libertarians such as Josiah Warren.

Alan Watts, writing about the difference between wealth and money, goes to the heart of the problem in the following story:

> Remember the Great Depression of the Thirties? One day there was a flourishing consumer economy, with everyone on the up-and-up; and the next: poverty, unemployment and breadlines. What happened? The physical resources of the country — the brain, brawn, and raw materials — were in no way depleted, but there was a sudden absence of money, a so-called financial slump. Complex reasons for this kind of disaster can be elaborated at lengths by experts in banking and high finance who cannot see the forest for the trees. But it was just as if someone had come to work on building a house and, on the morning of the Depression, the boss had to say, "Sorry, baby, but we can't build today. No inches." "Whaddya mean, no inches? We got wood. We got metal. We even got

tape measures." "Yeah, but you don't understand business. We been using too many inches, and there's just no more to go around."

A few years later, people were saying that Germany couldn't possibly equip a vast army and wage a war, because it didn't have enough gold.

Designing a system where gold and paper dollars mean less than sweat and natural resources and ingenuity will take a long time and a lot of experience. Without it, though, trade between neighborhoods won't be all that different from trade between "enlightened" corporations, or countries.

Communication is the key to all of this. Without the kind of communications which permit the average citizen to interrelate with other citizens, trade becomes the province of business people, politics is governed by representatives, and intercommunalism becomes much like internationalism; that is, relations between sovereign states, between diplomats who are emissaries of duly elected political leaders.

Face-to-face politics in neighborhood assemblies is one important form of communication. Reliance on friends and neighbors rather than remote bureaucrats or ideologies is another. It is possible now for entire neighborhoods to interact with one another even under current commercial restrictions. For a flat fee per month an organization in a neighborhood can buy a WATS (Wide Area Telephone Service) line. This gives unlimited telephone service to various parts of the country. (Note that the telephone company doesn't look kindly on buying WATS time and permitting average citizens to use it. The student government at the University of Colorado reportedly tried to buy a WATS line for use of the student body and was turned down. It would have been too much of a bargain.) Regular telephone service can be extended by attaching an amplifier to the phone and microphones in a large room. This permits groups of people to talk with other groups of people.

Short-wave radios are now comparatively inexpensive and a network of such units could provide a link among communities and help coordinate actions when necessary. On Thursdays, at 9

P.M., for example, the Soho neighborhood in New York City might gather in a room to talk with interested residents in a neighborhood in Tucson, Arizona. They could talk and trade information and experiences. And if there were need for an in-depth follow-up, they could rely on a long letter, or videotape.

Technical assistance can be transferred in this manner, at least on a preliminary level. One community which needed assistance in building a fish tank could get a videotape designed by another neighborhood about how they constructed their own system, accompanied with a manual of instructions.

Videotape is especially useful in establishing contacts between cultures. For example, a videotape could be filmed of a Chinese block association, with its members discussing how it operates, how jobs are established, what its relationship to higher levels of government are, etc. A translation could be dubbed or subtitled, and then shown in an American neighborhood, where the community's responses would be filmed, as well as a description or visualization of organizations in the neighborhood with similar functions. In this way experiences and ideas could be exchanged while maintaining cultural differences. It could establish direct communication between groups not previously having access to each other, such as farmers, workers, housewives, scientists, the unemployed.

People might at first trade ideas about their different social and economic forms. People have different visions of the future. China with its communal system; Yugoslavia with its worker-management in factories; Tanzania with its pragmatic approach to education; the United States with its highly sophisticated technology. New ideas and cultural concepts spread quickly throughout the world. Just as the idea of women's liberation spread quickly, so the idea of worker control or local self-reliance might have similar impact. Often people have difficulty understanding how things might look after a change. They cling to the present for fear of what disruptions might bring. With transnational communications systems they could begin to see not only how different systems work, but what a synthesis of different cultures might look like.

Finally, such links would begin to break down the inherent

apolitical nature of American neighborhoods and communities and begin to coordinate activities vis-à-vis larger institutions which can affect the survival of the community. We can use Chile under Salvador Allende as an example. In that country there was a race going on under Allende, a race between those on the local levels who were trying to construct political, social, and economic institutions as quickly as they could to maintain and solidify revolutionary change, and those international economic, military, and political forces which were trying to bring down the government by armed subversion, reduction of aid and credit and a cut-off of loans and imports. During this time there was almost no contact between those neighborhood organizations in Chile and budding organizations in the United States. Such contact could have at first been one of mutual curiosity, a trading of information about their different attitudes and cultures. Workers in Chile could have talked about self-management; women could discuss the different concepts in child rearing and day care in the two countries; musicians could have played their music or shown their art to one another. But, as friendships developed, the broader context of the dialogue could have been defined and developed. This probably would have come about quicker because of the kinds of people involved. Academicians can trade in ideas, but the average citizen likes to move quickly from gossip to personal needs. Fairly rapidly, one neighborhood might have learned that another was threatened by outside forces. And in many cases these forces might be similar. The neighborhood in Butte, Montana, fighting the mining under its ground might discover that a neighborhood in Chile is threatened by the same copper company's operations there. The neighborhood in New York City which could not get any bank money for home-ownership mortgages might learn that a Santiago neighborhood was starving because the First National City Bank had refused loans to underwrite purchase of international foodstuffs. Slogans, and rhetoric, and political labels quickly would change to the concrete realities of survival. As a result, one neighborhood might ask what the other needed. Chile might need spare parts, or medicine, or dollars. Both might need mutual support against external forces. The dynamic, based on nothing more exotic than personal communication controlled by the neighborhood itself, is very strong.

Eventually trade might begin to broaden. American concepts of low-scale technology could be linked up with the needs of Chilean neighborhoods. Israeli villages could supply needed know-how on solar systems. Swedish towns could provide knowledge about urban planning and sewerage systems. Chinese communes could teach how to make herbal medicines and institute nonhierarchical work structures, and so forth — an intercommunal pooling of information and technical and cultural assistance.

There is a further benefit that this kind of intercommunalism produces. It makes life in a neighborhood varied and exciting in a way that has not previously been the case. In many neighborhoods, as the old grow older and the young grow up, the sameness of the surroundings and the population, coupled with the innate conservatism of the older generation's culture, leads to boredom and a vague desire to travel to new places. This wanderlust, particularly on the part of the young, will never cease, and it is a beneficial thing. But the boredom can be partially overcome by bringing in new faces, new voices, new information, and new struggles. New friends, strange cultures, and a sense of mutual support and assistance can also aid tremendously in keeping the population of a neighborhood stable while its surroundings are exciting, changing, fresh, rewarding, fulfilling.

NINE

A Neighborhood of the Future

Elroy Jones woke up at nine o'clock, remembering once more the old days when he had to wake up hours earlier to beat the commuter traffic into town. While leisurely eating breakfast he savored the fine fruit that he had with his eggs. Both came from the greenbelt around the city which was established after the great famine of the late 1970s. Cliffdale, the neighborhood Elroy lived in, grew much of its own food. During the great famine, when the large food corporations forced out almost all the small family farmers, and then collapsed themselves, the neighborhood had gathered together to see how much food it could produce. It never amounted to more than twenty-five percent of its needs. Cliffdale was just too densely populated. But, when the famine hit, the neighborhood had to do something. The Cliffdale Community Council, which had been negotiating lethargically with the city authorities for more power over local affairs, began telling residents to take direct action, to tear up paved streets that weren't absolutely essential for traffic and bring topsoil from areas where there was a "surplus," like city woods. Garbage and human wastes were collected to provide compost and fertilizer, and within only one season the street gardens had borne vegetables.

As in any crisis, unity was strong during that time. The city tried to stop the actions at first, but held off when other neighborhoods began imitating Cliffdale's policies. "How the world changes," Elroy mused. He could still remember the 1950s and 1960s, when there was a rush to pave over the cities, a frenzy so great that even private citizens joined in, cementing over their backyards with terraces, covering their front yards with artificial grass.

Elroy went outside. He could easily walk to the community factory, where he worked assembling d.c. motors used in the electric cars which were everywhere in the community. But a light rain was falling and he decided to take the minibus system for those ten blocks. As he waited under the canopy for the bus, he glanced at the falling rain, glad that nature was providing for the sustenance of the neighborhood. Only a decade before rain was considered a nuisance in the cities. In fact, there had been one plan put forward by a famous futurist (how strange the word seemed now, when everyone considered themselves futurists) that cities cover themselves with huge domes to keep away the rain and snow. Elroy understood the argument for such a plan. It had even made sense at the time. With the city paved over there had been nothing to catch the water and it carried silt and leaf residue and auto exhaust to nearby water supplies, polluting them. In Washington, D.C., where Cliffdale was located, the combined sewer system had made it necessary to open the gates when it rained because rain overloaded the sewage capacity, causing raw sewage to pour directly into the Potomac River. And, besides, people had forgotten what rain was for. Bus stops had no canopies then. Driving was hazardous in the rain. Domes sounded like a pretty good idea.

The minibus quietly slid into the bus stop and Elroy got on. He joked some with Pat, the driver, retelling stories about the factory where they had recently worked together. Pat, like most people in the neighborhood, rotated through a number of jobs during his work lifetime. It had been discovered, by talking with workers, that they wanted three things. One was to control their work time, another was to have some feeling that they were making a whole product, some sense of craftsmanship. The third was that no one, not even on what some people would think was the best job of all, wanted to work at it for fifty years. So people tended to rotate. It has worked out pretty well, especially because people who worked at a number of jobs achieved an understanding of the pressures peculiar to each occupation.

Of course no system is ideal, Elroy thought, and this one still has its problems. Changing people's conceptions about employment was still going to take some time. For generations, even millennia, people worked so they could earn enough money to survive. The job, ideally, was interesting, but it was mainly a necessary evil used for supporting wife, family, and house. The idea that work should fill a social function, producing wealth for the community, was a relatively new concept. Elroy remembered the many experiments in resource allocation. The community, like many, had gone through a pro-Bellamy period, reverting to labor credits administered through a central office, but had found the system too favorable to a centralized state apparatus. They had tried time units, basing the cost of an item on the amount of labor that went into it. This was more comfortable, because people could intuitively accept the fact that forty hours of work was forty hours of work; in fact, if one were to judge by the physical effort involved, surely the construction worker was working harder than the bank president. In the final analysis time was the essential common denominator for all humanity. Presently Cliffdale was working with a hybridized system, using a free market and monetary incentive for luxury items, and a guaranteed goods level for anything else.

There had been a time when people had taken advantage of such a system, and there were still many neighborhoods that carried on with the old market economy because they had had such problems with free goods. But in most communities, after people got over their initial impulse to just sit and do nothing, new work ethics arose and people decided they were too bored just sitting around. Besides, when the choice was no longer working for forty or fifty hours a week at a menial job that one did not like and had no control over versus goofing off, but rather was a choice of twenty hours of work in a comfortable work environment with rotation of jobs and worker control, the whole appeal of work changed.

There still remained a few dirty jobs, but ingenuity had

eliminated many of them. At first the community councils had rotated the more unattractive jobs, so that garbage collection, for example, was done by one person for only one week out of the year. Soon the neighborhood decided that the goal should be to eliminate the job. The neighborhood outlawed most packaging, and prohibited the use of non-returnable containers. With in-house composting, garbage collection almost disappeared. The main item of collection currently was goods that had become worn out and newspapers, and even newspapers were diminishing as new electronic communication became more widespread and creative.

As the bus quietly moved along the city streets, Elroy remembered that in the old days the neighborhood had had almost twenty-five percent of its labor force unemployed. In fact, the figure was closer to forty percent when you counted all the women who were staying at home taking care of one child apiece. The process in the old society was to take more and more people out of the labor force and provide for their sustenance from those who were working. It seemed ridiculous now, but at the time it was common practice for children to go to school at the age of four, and stay there until the age of twenty-five, never performing any socially useful work in those twenty-one years, but rather "learning" in some strange, mystical way. They would then take a job, work for approximately thirty years and then retire on pensions. Those who were not so fortunate waited until age sixty and retired on social security. Some people had warned that this could not continue; even in the early 1960s there were voices of doom, but most of the attention was given to the prophets of plenty, who assured people that ever-expanding wealth would permit everyone to be taken care of. Ironically, it was money which was the underpinning and at the same time the burden of the system. The growth in those days caused a transiency in the population. Children no longer took care of their parents. Parents no longer took care of their children. Neighbors no longer talked with one another about disputes; they called the police. Families served very little of the traditional functions of education, protection, and acculturation. Children ran away from homes to be taken care of in runaway shelters. An increasing part of the population was in jail, or halfway houses.

Things that had been free no longer were. Disputes were often mediated by paid policemen and paid judges. Entertainment cost money. Old people were cared for in rest homes. All of this, plus the dwindling number of people who worked for a living, finally caused such a great strain on the system that people had to devise new ways of living. The first plans were no advance. They tried to get people to do menial work in return for welfare checks. The unemployed were set to work picking up garbage and beautifying streets. It didn't work because these underpaid laborers, working for government checks, began to compete with other paid workers, and added to the unemployment rolls.

Elroy wasn't sure what would have happened if the economy had not suddenly nosedived, throwing thousands out of work and abruptly terminating the growth spree of the 1960s. The depression forced stability on neighborhoods. People became less transient. They relied on each other more, not out of altruism but out of necessity. And, finally, new definitions of work and public welfare arose. The school systems taught students in the factories and the communities themselves. The difference between vocational and academic training disappeared as technicians, laborers, engineers, and others worked together to redesign the neighborhood itself. Day care centers flourished, with old people, who could recount the experiences of yesteryear, taking the main burden of caring for the children.

As the bus rolled on toward the factory, Elroy noticed the forest of windmills on the rooftops, but gave them no special attention, ignoring them much as his father would have ignored the forest of TV antennas on rooftops of his time. He saw the sun glinting off the solar cells and solar collectors and remembered suddenly the bitter arguments that had occurred when solar energy was first introduced. It seemed that no one had thought about "sun rights," that is, the right not to have a building go up next door which cut off one's access to a certain number of hours of sunlight a day. Under the old system, there were court suits and zoning-commission hearings, but in most cases the owners of high-rise office buildings and apartment houses won their case. When zoning was left to the neighborhood, however, this stopped, and right now the line of equal rooftops was unbroken. With the coming of local control there was a certain sameness in architecture, but this sameness was forced on the people by nature's laws. Windows faced to the south, as did slanted rooftops. The solar cells and collectors were combined. Someone in a neighborhood in France had discovered the way to most efficiently combine the heating and electrical solar equipment and that system was currently sweeping the world. Some fossil fuels were needed still to supplement sun and wind systems, but not much. Petroleum which had been used primarily in internal-combustion engines was now restricted by consent of all the people in the country to certain plastic materials and pharmaceuticals. It had taken a plague to convince people of that. In the late 1970s, with gasoline consumption still increasing, the cities ran out of energy-intensive chlorine supplies because it was not as profitable to supply the city water-purification system as it was to supply cars. As people began to get sick from drinking untreated water, the hospitals filled up, but there were not enough medicines available to treat the ill because so many of the medicines had a petroleum base. When the death toll ran into the thousands, people decided it was better to conserve the precious raw material for future generations' health and welfare than to burn it in inefficient car engines.

Transportation had become a much different affair in Cliffdale. Transportation systems that went from all areas of the city and suburbs to downtown had been pretty much done away with. Much of the transportation had been replaced by electronic communication of information. When the two-way communications systems had been installed in every home, and the waveguide systems had permitted the number of communications channels to be almost infinite in number, travel to downtown had diminished considerably. Most of the physical transportation had been useful only as a way to pass information along. The boss went downtown in order to spend most of the day in conference, dictating letters, or making phone calls. The secretary went downtown in order to type, answer the phone, and file correspondence. And so on. It seemed almost a miracle when someone suggested that an effective electronic communication system would pay for itself in less than a year, by saving on travel expenses and deterioration of office buildings, not to mention wear and tear on nerves.

When electronic communication freed people up, patterns of living began to change. Families could once more stay at home together. Initially there were many who left the cities altogether, to live in isolated rural areas, doing their jobs by cathode-ray-computer screen and video phone. Some still stayed in those remote areas, but fairly soon people discovered that there was a need for physical presence, at least in social activities, that human beings are gregarious and that communicating by electronics was psychologically debilitating.

When downtown became only an electronic pulse away, rather than an hour by freeway during rush hour, the sense of the city quietly altered. Factories were established in the neighborhoods. Transportation systems became locally oriented. It seemed ridiculous to think that in the old days it was easier to get downtown, a distance of some ten miles, than it was to go sideways to another neighborhood, a distance of half a mile. Now the minibuses, the electric cars which were rented, not owned, by the neighborhood residents, and the bicycles took care of local transportation.

Elroy disembarked at the factory, a warehouse that had been used at one time to store office supplies. As he walked into the assembly area he noticed a group of co-workers gathered around a large TV screen. Walking over to them he saw that they were talking with workers in Sweden who had just discovered a more efficient method of manufacturing the d.c. motors which were the main product of the factory. Sven Palmer, a young electrician working in the Swedish factory, had developed a way of winding the armature which increased efficiency by almost ten percent. He was busy demonstrating the new winding technique to the American workers. Elizabeth Rhodes was the first to get the knack of it and a cheer went up from the workers gathered around the screen when they realized that one more transfer of technology from people to people had been accomplished.

Realizing that the increased efficiency would produce a

savings for the community, the workers decided to declare a holiday. In the old days an increase in efficiency of the product would probably have been ignored, and any increase in production techniques meant more products coming off the line in less time. Products were made to break quickly, for in the sales of parts and new products lay the profits of the firm. In Cliffdale the community decided how many d.c. motors it needed, and then worked long enough to produce that many. There were always some new ones needed, and there were also replacements needed. Whenever there was a breakthrough such as had happened today, the old motors were taken in and rebuilt to increase their efficiency. But the factory would never produce more than was needed. So in this case an increase in efficiency probably meant a decrease in work hours. A celebration was in order, a holiday declared.

Elroy recalled, with pleasure, that the very television screen that had enabled them to learn the new armature winding had been built by a previous work group in the neighborhood which had done its work so well that it hadn't reconvened now for more than a year. Only its small transistor production unit, housed in the top floor of a building once used for real-estate speculators' offices, was active regularly. The holiday declared when the television production had been completed had been something special because it was accompanied by a neighborhood meeting in which it was decided that three people from the neighborhood would, voluntarily, of course, take a year away from the neighborhood to work at the regional facility where, by intercommunity agreement, TV transmission equipment was built and this area's participation in the global interneighborhood TV network maintained.

This holiday, Elroy thought, they might take some time also to decide who wanted to work for a much shorter period of time on the installation, by community cooperative effort, of a new diesel electric power plant in the locomotive used to maintain rail service between the towns of the Atlantic seaboard with whom Cliffdale joined in a transportation pool.

Elroy's own inclination at this point was to think more about a project far, far different from his usual activity, to satisfy his own need and desire for at least a short time of active life away from the community. Some people never left the community. Others were away almost half their lives, making it hard sometimes to regard them as resident in any one place. Elroy was inclined to stay put himself, but to enjoy a week away now and then.

Life used to be rigorously divided between work, travel, toil and pleasure. Now it wasn't. It didn't have to be and no one in his right mind would want it to be, Elroy thought. Why had so many people put up with it for so long, he wondered. Histories have many answers but, obviously, he thought, the most reasonable ones had to do with the control of productive and natural resources by so few people, the absence of a truly free society in which people generally, and not a few in particular, used their own good common sense to make the decisions affecting their lives.

At any rate, what Elroy had been thinking about lately was signing up for one of the still vacant volunteer spots in the regional iron-ore cooperative, to do a week of mining. He'd hate to do such work day in and day out, of course, but for a short period it was bracing, helped restore some of the muscular vigor that too much time at an indoor job was bound to sap, and put him directly in touch with new people in a new environment.

Actually, the neighborhood was rather sharply divided on the matter of iron ore this year. The neighborhood's own amazingly successful recycling efforts had meant that iron and steel supplies (remelted in a solar-powered refractory furnace) were more than enough for the neighborhood's current production plans. There was a strong feeling that the figures on need projected by some were too high. At any rate, the neighborhood assembly had been unable to come anywhere near a consensus on the matter, there was no widespread spirit in the neighborhood for volunteering and the matter now rested solely and informally with individuals who could, if they wanted, volunteer for the iron mining — or just forget it. (If the assembly *had* agreed, then there would have been neighborhood meetings, recruiting festivals, and public commendation for those who went.)

Elroy was persuaded that, overall, it would be better to step up ore production right now rather than wait until the needs were more apparent. Also, he had to confess to himself, he just plain welcomed a chance to get away for a while and to do some hard work. It would be a real vacation.

Meanwhile, Elroy joined Elizabeth in walking down to the day-care center to see her two children, ages two and three. The brightly painted, multi-colored exterior was a far cry from the gray façade that had greeted the visitor a decade before. At that time it had been a bank, one of five in the neighborhood. As Cliffdale established its own bank and credit union and people began to put their money in that institution, the other branch banks moved out of the neighborhood to more profitable areas. The high-ceilinged banking area provided a perfect play area for children, with ladders and swings, and even sandboxes ingeniously built in. As Elizabeth and Elroy came into the building, they were greeted by the subdued rumble of forty children at play, painting, drawing, dancing, clowning around.

Most working parents visited their children at some time during the day, every day. Some parents, of course, elected to stay full time with their children, but few did so in isolation — working at a day-care center being a far more pleasurable answer than staying cooped up in a small house. Nursing mothers established a schedule after the first few months of feeding their children. But the everyday care was given over to those in the community who were most interested in children, who were patient, and who had some experience. The staff here were studying child psychology also in the local community college. Some would help in setting up new centers where the need arose. It had been discovered shortly after the day-care center opened that old people enjoyed very much sitting in the building and watching the children, and that the children enjoyed that attention. The tradition of story telling had been revived by old-timers who knew about the old days in ways that TV and radio didn't seem to capture.

As with most buildings in the community, this one was multi-purpose. There was a laundromat in the basement (with its waste heat used to heat the day-care center in winter). There was a lounge for the elderly and infirm. And there was a library-communication facility where people could browse through literature or use video channels to hook up with other communities or individuals around the world.

The idea, fairly successful at this point, was to bring the community together, especially those segments that had been isolated. Community centers had been the refuge of the young, the teenagers, replete with pool tables and bowling alleys or stages. The old were segregated in rest homes, the very young in nurseries. Just as the food market in Cliffdale was located very near the factories and schools, so this building housed different projects and activities to reduce the compartmentalizing that society had fallen into before.

Elizabeth took her two children out of the building, after checking with the supervisor on duty. It was late afternoon, and they would be going home soon in any case. The children loved to pick vegetables so Elroy and Elizabeth went over to the garden their block used for growing their food. Probably a visitor to the neighborhood would have found the proliferation of greenhouses and vegetables and fruit trees the most awesome sight in the community. Although Cliffdale did not grow all its food within its borders, it seemed that everywhere one turned there were ripe tomatoes, or huge cabbages, or the beginnings of pumpkins. The children loved the pumpkins best, besides the sunflowers, and probably for the same reason — they were so big.

As the children played Elroy and Elizabeth talked about the years immediately ahead for the children when they would move from the day-care center to whichever educational or apprenticeship pattern seemed best in light of their own temperaments, of their parents' inclinations, or even of the decisions of their friends in the current center. Since the society was free, since the neighborhood was, indeed, sovereign over itself and its resources, and since it was no longer necessary to beat down your neighbors in order to get what you wanted out of life (assuming that the "want" didn't include raw power or some sadistic desire to push people around), since, in short, the purpose of community was the well-being of its members rather than the profit of absentee owners, the early educational decisions of children were nowhere near as binding or formative as in the past.

People could always change these days. Opportunities were, in effect, endless, work was honored, waste was shunned, cooperation was the way of the world and competition was reserved just for gala events such as music festivals, art shows, and the many trade and craft fairs at which people vied, but lovingly, to show the excellence of their work.

The real difference was that to be a winner, now, there did not have to be losers.

The honor was in the trying. Excellence was freely admitted and admired without resentment and jealousy — everybody's reward, ultimately, being the same: work done as well as one could, whether a new process for suspending a bridge, or a poem.

Knowledge for the new life had become, simply, knowledge for life. Manipulative skills, the skills of exploitation and advantage, of wile and conniving, were no longer respected. There were no institutions to teach them. Schools, even university communities, formed now to engage people, teachers and students, senior and junior scholars, everyone involved, in processes of exploring knowledge of the natural world and the ethics of the human world in that nature.

For many young people this meant, mainly, joining the mainstream of the community as early as possible, becoming responsible and self-reliant young people. Basic skills, such as reading, rudimentary science, logic, knowledge of the ways of the neighborhood and of surrounding communities, were taught everywhere: in the day-care centers, at home, in groups that children formed themselves.

Other and more special skills — arts, crafts, specific sciences — could be approached in several ways. The neighborhood itself had formed an ongoing educational community for electrodynamics, an area that over time had become particularly important in this particular neighborhood. Senior skilled people, in this community, volunteered to work for certain times each day with young people interested in the subject, emphasizing the theoretical knowledge which, as soon as possible, would be given practical application in part-time apprenticeships to people actually working at production or research. Age was simply no longer a criterion for what a young person should do at any particular point. Skill, personal devotion, and direction were the measures now.

And, quite importantly, from the time a young person was accepted into full citizenship of the neighborhood assembly (the young person's neighbors applied for her or him, the assembly voted approval or not), the young person was fully participating in all the decisions not only of education and apprenticeship but of everything affecting the life of the neighborhood.

Elroy and Elizabeth had first met during the years of hottest debate over the nature of the assembly. Elroy had insisted then that the assembly needed to be subordinated to an executive council of key people who could direct the energies of the neighborhood. Elizabeth wisely, Elroy now happily admitted, had held out for the full sovereignty of the assembly and for the notion that only a fully self-reliant and self-responsible community could realize all the potential of its members, that any hard-and-fast delegations of responsibility to some just weakened the responsibility of the rest. That idea had prevailed and the neighborhood now was fully free because the citizens were fully involved and fully responsible.

Beyond the neighborhood, of course, there also was a political life, but even it was carefully guarded so that power would never again, as it had in the past, accumulate in a few hands.

Elroy was a member of the city-wide council which did planning on a larger scale than the neighborhood. Each neighborhood controlled its own affairs. The city-wide council was made up of representatives chosen by the neighborhoods. All the members were subject to recall and, in fact, a parliamentary system had developed whereby, if the representative found that a majority of his or her constituents disagreed with a decision, he or she resigned pending a vote of confidence. The city-wide council had control over those areas of planning which did not lend themselves to just neighborhood decision making. For example, the creation of greenbelts, the discussion of basic manufacturing resources, the placement of hospitals, were all under the province of the city-wide council. Usually the city council made tentative decisions, for example, deciding how many hospitals were needed for a city of 500,000, and then the neighborhoods thrashed out where they would be located. Every neighborhood had its own clinics, which, by the way, also were multipurpose, hooked up with the food markets, the links between nutrition and health.

Meetings were at a different neighborhood every month and were held once a week. Not very many people showed up unless there was a crisis period. Participation occurred as people felt decisions *had* to be made, or when decisions had to be *unmade*.

Now, the children were running back to Elizabeth and Elroy. The growing field they had just left was gleaming in the late sun. Friends, neighbors, passed them, each with a greeting. Friends, neighbors, working at other times at freely chosen tasks, each with a productive place in the community — to feed it, provide its material needs, delight it, decorate it, enrich it in some way.

No wasted materials littered the common walkways. The air was clear. People did not fear one another. The most respected were not the most powerful but the most creative and the most cooperative. Art flourished as the creative practice of the entire community. Some excelled. All participated. Music was the common delight of the community. Science was the common knowledge, letting everyone live in nature knowing of its and their limits as well as possibilities. Women, children, men, the aged, the idiosyncratic were kind to one another, bound together not by laws but by their common human condition.

The laughter of the children glided like a stream of tiny bells through the neighborhood. Dusk was nearing. And tomorrow was beginning to form in the neighborhood once again.

Bibliography

Chapter 2   Developing Neighborhood Awareness: The First Institutions

Alinsky, Saul, *Reveille for Radicals* (New York: Vintage, 1969).

Applebaum, Richard P., "Community Control in Isla Vista: Some Prospects for Self-Government" in *Working Papers*, 1, no. 2 (Summer 1973).

Nasa, David, ed., *Starting Your Own High School: Elizabeth Cleaners Street School* (New York: Random House, 1972).

Evans, E. Belle, Beth Shub, and Marlene Weinstein, *Day Care: How to Plan, Develop and Operate a Day Care Center* (Boston: Beacon, 1971).

Fairchild, Richard, ed., *Utopia, USA: Writings on Contemporary Alternative Life Styles* (San Francisco: Alternatives Foundation, 1972).

Graubard, Allen, *Free the Children: Radical Reform and the Free School Movement* (New York: Vintage, 1973).

The Great Atlantic and Pacific School Conspiracy, *Doing Your Own School: A Practical Guide to Starting and Operating a Community School* (Boston: Beacon, 1972).

Jones, W. Ron, *Finding Community: A Guide to Community Research and Action* (Palo Alto, Calif.: James E. Freel and Associates, 1971).

Kahn, Si, *How People Get Power: Organizing Oppressed Communities for Action* (New York: McGraw-Hill, 1970).

Margolies, Richard, "Coming Together — the Co-operative Way" in *New Leader*, April 17, 1972; available from North American Student Cooperative Association.

National Free Clinic Movement: Historical Perspective (San Francisco: Haight-Ashbury Publications).

Warren, Roland L., *Studying Your Community* (Glencoe, Ill.: Free Press, 1955).

Chapter 3   *Controlling the Local Economy: The Growth of Community Businesses*

Clark, Steve, *Washington Food Federation, Alternative Food System Development Program: A Proposal* (Washington, D.C.: Stone Soup).

Constant, Florence, *Community Development Corporations: An Annotated Bibliography* (Cambridge, Mass.: Center for Community Economic Development).

Cooperatives in Agribusiness, Farmer Cooperative Services, U.S. Department of Agriculture, educational circular 33, Oct. 1972.

Direct Charge Cooperatives: An Evaluation (Ashby, Mass.: International Independence Institute).

Food Conspiracy Newsletter.

Food Cooperatives: How to Start One and Make It Prosper (Philadelphia: Food Conspiracies).

Knapp, Joseph G., *The Advance of American Cooperative Enterprise* (Danville, Ill.: Interstate Printers and Publishers).

Krishan, Gopi, *Consumer Group Legal Services* (Washington, D.C.: Cooperative League of the USA, 1973).

Panford, Art, *Co-op Depots: Reasons for, Principles, Methods, Materials* (Washington, D.C.: Cooperative League of the USA, 1970).

Ronco, William, *Food Co-ops: An Alternative to Shopping in Supermarkets* (Boston: Beacon, 1974).

————— "The New Food Co-ops: Making of a Movement?" in *Working Papers*, 1, no. 1 (Spring 1973).

Stein, Barry, *How Successful Are CDC's? An Interim Report* (Cambridge, Mass.: Center for Community Economic Development, 1973).

Warbase, James Peter, ed., *Consumer Cooperation and the Society of the Future* (New York: Consumers Cooperative Publishing Association, 1969).

Chapters 4 and 5   *Controlling the Local Economy* and *Neighborhood Housing*

Brugmann, Bruce, Greggar Slettleland, and *Bay Guardian* staff, *The Ultimate Highrise* (San Francisco: 1971).

Communities/Housing: Source Catalog No. 2 (Chicago: Swallow, 1972).

The Community Land Trust: A Guide to a New Model for Land Tenure in America (Cambridge, Mass.: Center for Community Economic Development and the International Independence Institute).

Goodman, Emily Jane, *Tenant Survival Book* (Indianapolis, Ind.: Bobbs-Merrill, 1972).

Gottschalk, Shimon, *Community Based Welfare* (Ashby, Mass.: International Independence Institute).

Kirshner, Ed, *A Housing Proposal* (Oakland, Calif.: Community Ownership Organizing Project).

Morey, James L. and Mel Epstein, *Housing Development: A Tool for Community Economic Development in Low Income Areas* (Cambridge, Mass.: Center for Community Economic Development).

National Credit Union Administration, *Annual Report; The Federal Credit Union Act and Related Statutes;* and *Federal Credit Union By-Laws.*

Neighborhood Development Corporation: A Business Proposal (Chicago: Adlai Stevenson Institute, 1972); also available from Center for Community Change.

People Before Property: A Real-Estate Primer and Research Guide (Cambridge, Mass.: Urban Planning Aid, Inc.).

Simpson, Chris, *This Is Not a History Book: A Brief History of Sustaining Funds* (Washington, D.C., Common Sense).

Smith, Herbert H., *The Citizen's Guide to Zoning* (West Trenton, N.J.: Chandler Davis Publishing Company, 1972).

Tenants' Handbook: Legal Tactics (Cambridge, Mass.: Tenants Organizing Committee, 1973).

Chapter 6   Neighborhood Government

Borosage, Robert, *A Sample Charter for McKees Rocks Borough or Stow Township* (Washington, D.C.: Institute for Neighborhood Studies, 1974).

Community Governance Study: Bibliography on Citizen Participation, Decentralization, and Services (Washington, D.C.: Institute for Local Self-Reliance, 1970).

Kotler, Milton, *Neighborhood Government: The Local Foundations of Political Life* (Indianapolis, Ind.: Bobbs-Merrill, 1969).

————*On Municipal Liberty: The Case of Boston* (Washington, D.C.: Institute for Neighborhood Studies).

Chapter 7   Neighborhood Production: The Limits of Self-sufficiency

Alternative Sources of Energy Magazine.

Blair, John, *Economic Concentration: Structure, Behavior, and Public Policy* (New York: Harcourt, Brace, Jovanovich, 1972).

Bookchin, Murray, *The Limits of the City* (New York: Harper & Row paperback orig., 1973).

————*Post-Scarcity Anarchism* (Berkeley, Calif.: Ramparts Press, 1971).

Eccli, Sandy, ed., *Alternative Sources of Energy: Practical Technology and Philosophy for a Decentralized Society* (Milaca, Minn.: Alternative Sources of Energy).

Goodman, Paul and Percival, *Communitas* (New York: Vintage, 1960).

Growth Industries and Project Selection: An Introduction for Community Development Corporations (Cambridge, Mass.: Center for Community Economic Development, 1971).

How to Survey Your Neighborhood's Food Growing Potential (Washington, D.C.: Institute for Local Self-Reliance).

New Alchemy Institute Journal.

Papanek, Victor, *Design for the Real World* (New York: Pantheon, 1971); also in Bantam paperback.

People for Self-Management Newsletter.

Schumacher, E. F., *Small Is Beautiful* (New York: Harper Torchbooks, 1973).

Stein, Barry, *The Community Context of Economic Conversion* (Cambridge, Mass.: Center for Community Economic Development, Nov. 1971).

Resource Directory

Adlai Stevenson Institute of International Affairs
5757 S. Woodlawn Ave.
Chicago, Ill. 60637

Alternatives Foundation
P.O. Drawer A
Diamond Heights Station
San Francisco, Calif. 94131

Alternative Sources of Energy
Rt. 2, Box 90A
Milaca, Minn. 56353

Cambridge Tenants Organizing Committee
Room 201
595 Massachusetts Ave.
Cambridge, Mass. 02139

Center for Community Change
1000 Wisconsin Ave. NW
Washington, D.C. 20007

Center for Community Economic Development
1878 Massachusetts Ave.
Cambridge, Mass. 02140

Common Sense
1802 Belmont Rd. NW
Washington, D.C. 20009

Community Ownership Organizing Project
349 62nd St.
Oakland, Calif. 94618

Consumers Cooperative Publishing Association
473 F.D.R. Drive
New York, N.Y. 10002

Cooperative League of the USA
1828 L. St. NW
Washington, D.C. 20036

Chandler Davis Publishing Company
Box 36
West Trenton, N.J. 08628

Farmer Cooperative Services
U.S. Department of Agriculture
Washington, D.C. 20250

Food Conspiracies
165 W. Harvey St.
Philadelphia, Penna. 19144

Food Conspiracy Newsletter
412 N. 4th Ave.
Tucson, Ariz. 85705

James E. Freel and Associates
577 College Ave.
Palo Alto, Calif. 94306

Haight-Ashbury Publications
P.O. Box 27278
San Francisco, Calif. 94127

Institute for Local Self-Reliance
1717 18th St. NW
Washington, D.C. 20009

Institute for Neighborhood Studies
1520 New Hampshire Ave. NW
Washington, D.C. 20036

International Independence Institute
West Road, Box 183
Ashby, Mass. 01431

Interstate Printers and Publishers
Danville, Ill.

National Credit Union Administration
Washington, D.C. 20456

New Alchemy Institute
Shank's Pond Road
Falmouth, Mass. 02540

North American Student Cooperative Association
2546 Student Activities Building
Ann Arbor, Mich. 48104

People for Self-Management Newsletter
Professor Jarek
Cornell University
Ithaca, N.Y. 14850

Stone Soup
18th & S St. NW
Washington, D.C. 20009

Swallow Press, Inc.
1139 S. Wabash Ave.
Chicago, Ill. 60605

Urban Planning Aid, Inc.
639 Massachusetts Ave.
Cambridge, Mass. 02139